KNOCKING

ON

DOORS,

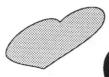

OPENING

HEARTS

RALPH W. NEIGHBOUR, JR.

This equipping guide is designed for use by cell group churches. It assumes the cells are called "Shepherd Groups, " and that group members are being equipped at varying levels of ministry. For further information, read *Where Do We Go From Here?* This handbook for developing cell group churches may be ordered from the address below.

KNOCKING ON DOORS, OPENING HEARTS
Second Edition

Published by Touch Outreach Ministries, Inc.
P. O. Box 19888
Houston, TX 77224, USA
(713) 497 7901

Printed in the Republic of Singapore
By BAC Printers

9876543 m

TABLE OF CONTENTS

 # ACKNOWLEDGEMENTS

To G. P. Rockwell, who taught me at age 15 that a burdened heart is a broken heart, and that "sales pitches" for the Gospel message are a shabby substitute for authentic, Spirit-led harvesting.

To those scores of unbelievers I have shared with, who confirmed over and over that helping someone receive Christ as Savior and Lord requires the Gospel to be "fleshed out" by believers who *show* before they *tell*.

To R. C. Smith, for his presentation of John 3:16 and the diagram used with it. We were both astonished when we discovered how closely what he had developed, incorporated into this manual, paralleled the MASTER PLAN, used for years in my *TOUCH BASIC TRAINING*. Those who continue their equipping by taking that course after becoming proficient in this one will find it easy to expand their harvesting skills.

To you, dear reader, for your hungry heart and your desire to be used in fields "white unto harvest" all around you. As you go in pairs from your Shepherd Group to meet with searching hearts, you may be certain your Lord will empower you for your tasks.

Finally, to the *searching ones,* as they are filled with the joy of their salvation when the owners of this manual lead you to Christ.

If not before then, I'll meet you at His throne!

Ralph W. Neighbour, Jr.

BEFORE YOU BEGIN...

This manual will equip you to minister to unbelievers and others who have visited gatherings of your cell church. Along with your partner, you will be ambassadors to them from your Shepherd Group. You will seek to bring those you contact into its love and nurture as soon as possible, and to bring unbelievers to accept Christ as Lord.

Visiting for the Lord isn't *taught*—it's *caught*. Hopefully, your partner has already studied this manual while visiting with a former partner, and will now become your "Equipper." He or she will review one Unit a week with you. There's a special section in the back of this book for the two of you to use in your review times.

EACH ONE TEACHES ONE, AFTER BEING TAUGHT BY ONE

After you have completed this manual, your present partner will go on to become a Share Group intern, and you'll be encouraged to equip and visit with a new partner. As you further develop this ministry with your intern, you'll discover the immense value of sharing what you have learned! Your journey into ministry will always be most meaningful when you follow the principle above: *"each one teaches one, after being taught by one."*

After each thought in your study, there's a "self test" section for you to complete. Don't skip over them! Use a pen to mark your answers. You'll share them with your "Equipper." These sections use this type face, and have a bar on the left side of the page. Sometimes there will be a box to check:

☐ **Go ahead: check inside this box now.**

☐ **Self test sections will help me retain what I am reading.**

ON THIS STAGE OF YOUR JOURNEY, YOU'LL LEARN TO...

1. Make telephone calls to persons who have visited the public meetings of your cell group church;

2. Make appropriate visits to them, ministering in the power of Christ;

3. Share your personal faith with them;

4. Explain the plan of salvation, using John 3:16 and a unique diagram built upon it;

5. Use the various printed materials provided for you to use as you visit;

6. Pray effectively for those you meet who face deep crises in their personal lives.

UNIT ONE
WHY DO WE VISIT?

The Biblical Basis for Visiting

Visiting those who visit your Celebrations or Congregation meetings is the first way your Shepherd Group says *"We care about you!"*

You never know what high drama will unfold as you make a first visit!

You'll meet *searching* hearts who are seeking to find peace of mind.

You'll find *torn* hearts that are bleeding, and need to be mended.

You'll find *hungry* hearts, starved for true community.

You'll find *loving* hearts, ready to be involved in the servant lifestyle of your Shepherd Group.

After making a few visits with me, one young Christian said, "Watching television is a waste of time. This has made me realize there's high drama everywhere...and God's power is *always* adequate to meet the needs we face. I'm glad I learned how to touch other people's lives!"

Jesus intended for us to continually widen our circle of ministry. There's no more powerful way to do so than by constantly making contacts with new people. Let's meditate on some scriptures which will help us realize the importance of making contacts with those who visit a public meeting of our cell group church. Read this scripture, called "The Great Commission," asking yourself if it refers to *you*, or only to Christians who are "different" from you:

And Jesus came up and spoke to them, saying, "All authority has been given to Me in heaven and on earth. Go therefore and make disciples of all the nations, baptizing them in the name of the Father and of the Son and the Holy Spirit, teaching them to observe all that I commanded you; and lo, I am with you always, even to the end of the age."
• Matthew 28:18-20

Is this verse a universal commission, or does it apply only to "special" Christians who are given a "special" calling?
(CHECK THE BOX OF YOUR CHOICE!)

☐   It's universal. Jesus commissioned every Christian.

☐   It's not universal...refers to "special" Christians.

Are you included in Jesus' commission?

☐   Yes

☐   Unsure

If you answered "unsure," consider this scripture:

But you are a chosen race, a royal priesthood, a holy nation, a people for God's own possession, that you may proclaim the excellencies of Him who has called you out of darkness into His marvelous light... • I Peter 2:9

Is this verse referring to every single believer, or only a select few?

☐   It's universal. If you're a Christian, you're included.

☐   It's not universal...refers to "special" Christians.

Are YOU included among those who are to "proclaim the excellencies of Him who has called you"?

And He said to them, "Thus it is written, that the Christ should suffer and rise again from the dead the third day; and that repentance for forgiveness of sins should be proclaimed in His name to all the nations, beginning from Jerusalem. You are witnesses of these things. And behold, I am sending the promise of my Father upon you . . ." • Luke 24:46-49

This scripture passage gives us our specific assignment...to be "witnesses" of Christ suffering and rising again, and that all men can receive forgiveness if they will turn away from their present lifestyles. Which of the statements below explain the meaning of being a "witness?"

☐ **You share something you have personally experienced.**

☐ **You share a truth you have not experienced.**

A witness is "one who bears evidence." It's sharing what you have personally experienced, or have personally observed in the lives of others who are Christians!

Next, consider this passage about the exclusiveness of the truth we are to present:

And there is salvation in no one else; for there is no other name under heaven that has been given among men, by which we must be saved. • Acts 4:12

If you meet people who say, "I already have a religion," are they exempt from the clear teaching of this verse?

☐ **Yes**

☐ **No**

Later in your training, you will learn that this powerful truth is at the heart of your sharing with others...but you can't persuade people to abandon their present beliefs by arguing with them, or by criticizing their religion. *Whenever you do so, you fail your Lord!* **Always, always remember: loving words attract; critical words** *repel.*

You may have been told by someone that God goes through the human race selecting special people to become His children...and that you can't expect all unbelievers to be received by Him, even if they have a desire to become Christians. Consider this verse:

> *This is good and acceptable in the sight of God our Savior, who desires all men to be saved and to come to the knowledge of the truth. For there is one God, and one mediator also between God and men, the man Christ Jesus, who gave Himself as a ransom for all...* • *I Timothy 2:3-6*

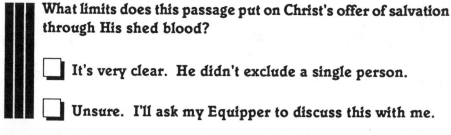

What limits does this passage put on Christ's offer of salvation through His shed blood?

☐ **It's very clear. He didn't exclude a single person.**

☐ **Unsure. I'll ask my Equipper to discuss this with me.**

Are your knees knocking? Are you saying to yourself, "I am a shy person, a private person. I don't enjoy meeting new people and getting acquainted with strangers. If contacting these people will require me to do something that's not natural for me to do, I don't know if I can go through with this. What should I do about my problem?" Read this next verse...

> *"...but you shall receive power when the Holy Spirit has come upon you; and you shall be My witnesses both in Jerusalem, and in all Judea and Samaria, and even to the remotest part of the earth."* • *Acts 1:8*

A TRUE STORY...
Sammy was a shy guy. He married Karen, also quiet and soft spoken. When they first attended a shepherd group, they agreed in advance they wouldn't return if they didn't feel comfortable around the other members. They were pleased when they realized they weren't expected to act like extroverts. After a couple of gatherings, both of them discovered the Lord was using them in special ways. Karen felt a deep desire to pray for a woman in the group who was suffering from postpartum depression. In her own quiet way, she poured

out her heart for her in a one-on-one prayer time. Sammy's "breakthrough" came when he sensed the Lord had given him a special word from Psalm 62:2 for a man in the group who had lost his job. In those first weeks in their Shepherd Group, they regularly discovered Christ empowering them for ministries—in ways that were perfectly natural for them. Their Shepherd explained to them that they were learning to exercise their spiritual gifts, and praised them for the spiritual growth they were experiencing. When the time came for them to take *this* course, Sammy said to Karen, "God made us to be the way we are. The same power of God's Spirit we've experienced in our shepherd group will flow through us when we go to visit new people. *As long as we're naturally letting Christ's power flow through us as we visit, we'll be effective.*"

List three times when Christ's power stimulated you to minister to someone else in your Shepherd Group:

1. _____

2. _____

3. _____

Can you expect Him to do the same kinds of things when He flows through you as you visit new people in their homes?

☐ Obviously, yes!

☐ Unsure. I'll ask my Equipper to discuss this with me.

The "Two by Two Pattern"

Six months prior to His death, Jesus turned His attention to a district East of the Jordan River, called Perea. It was a neglected area, ignored by the religious leaders of his day. He described Perea as a place where sheep had no shepherd! He planned to touch it with His love. To do so, He sent thirty-five teams to represent Him there. What they were told to do is exactly what you and your partner will be doing in the weeks ahead.

Read Jesus' commission to them:

Now after this the Lord appointed seventy others, and sent them two and two ahead of Him to every city and place where He Himself was going to come. And He was saying to them, "The harvest is plentiful, but the laborers are few; therefore beseech the Lord of the harvest to send out laborers into His harvest. Go your ways; behold, I send you out as lambs in the midst of wolves. Carry no purse, no bag, no shoes; and greet no one on the way. And whatever house you enter, first say, 'Peace be to this house.' And if a man of peace is there, your peace will rest upon him; but if not, it will return to you." • Luke 10:1-6

WHY DO YOU THINK JESUS SENT THEM IN PAIRS?

- Their relationship to each other as Christians would be unique. It alone would be a powerful witness to those they met in Perea.

- They would use their spiritual gifts to build up each other. Together, they would manifest God's power flowing through them as they prayed for the sick, the hurting, and the broken hearted.

- They would be able to share a common prayer life as they offered their peace to those they met—some who would respond, and some who would ridicule.

WHY DO YOU THINK JESUS TOLD THEM THEY WERE TOTALLY DEFENSELESS?

- They had to remember He was the Shepherd, their only protection against those who would attack them.

WHY DO YOU THINK HE TOLD THEM TO CARRY NO PURSE, BAG, OR SHOES?

- They were not going to cure social problems with welfare. The *power of Christ* would be given to them, and with it they would manifest the ability of God to change impossible situations.

A TRUE STORY...

Samuel Raj was the first man to graduate from Columbia Biblical Seminary with a Doctor of Ministries degree. He is from the South of India, an area filled with Hindu villages where the Gospel had never been shared. When he enters a town for the first time, he visits each home. Soon, he finds a serious problem—a very ill person, or perhaps an individual suffering from demonic oppression. He fasts and prays until the person is touched by the mighty power of Christ and made whole. The astonished villagers then gather around him, asking to know more about his God. Samuel then teaches from the Bible until they understand what it means to become Christians. He remains until a new work is established, and then moves on to do the same thing in the next village.

WHY DO YOU THINK HE TOLD THEM TO ENTER EACH HOME, MEET EACH PERSON, AND SEARCH FOR A "MAN OF PEACE?"

- The term *"man of peace"* means literally, *"a man who is searching for peace."*

- The person you visit may not be responsive to the message you bring. However, that person is a part of a "household" *(in Greek, the word is "oikos").* That first person may only be the means God has provided for you to meet a truly responsive person within the household. Therefore, don't just meet *one* person in a household—*meet every person!* Offer Christ's peace to *each one* as the Lord provides opportunities to do so.

YOU ARE ENCOURAGED TO SEARCH FOR THE "MAN OF PEACE!"

People constantly come to your public cell church services looking for God's plan for their lives. God has called us to reach out to every such person quickly. Remember: those who take the time to visit our services are searching for something they don't possess. You have the privilege of becoming Christ's ambassador to bring them to Him!

VISITATION CONTACTS INCLUDE THESE PERSONS:

1. Fellow Christians, looking for a way to follow the Master.
2. Fellow Christians, facing a deep crisis.
3. Fellow Christians, inactive and unmotivated.
4. Members of denominations, bored and looking around.
5. Curious persons, responding to bits of information about the work.
6. Unbelievers, searching for God and for meaning in life.
7. Unbelievers, brought to our fellowship by a friend.

This list is just a start. There are many more possibilities... Can you add two more possibilities to the list?

8. _____

9. _____

THESE ARE THE GUIDELINES FOR MAKING YOUR FIRST VISIT TO A PERSON WHO HAS VISITED YOUR PUBLIC SERVICES:

1. **Meet everyone in the house,** not just the person who scheduled the appointment. This includes children! The Lord has something in mind by sending you to make this visit. Pray earnestly you will be able to be His ambassador to all you meet.

2. **Be a learner!** What are the interests of these family members? Are there trophies on the mantle, certificates or guns on the wall? Can you discern a value system? Are there antiques, or is their furniture very simple? Is the house "lived in," or flawlessly clean?

3. **Get acquainted** with one another by sharing answers together to the "Quaker Questions:"

   - Where did we live between the ages of 7 and 12, and how many brothers and sisters were there in our families?
   - What kind of transportation did our families use back then?
   - Who was the person we felt closest to during those years?
   - When did God become more than a word to us? *(Give your own testimony at this time. It will be natural to do so!)*

4. **Seek to establish a bond of love** and respect for one another. At the same time, determine the special needs or interests of the people you are sharing with.

5. **Find a mutual area of interest,** or a need in your life or theirs, which would make it a natural thing to get together for a longer visit in the near future. Make an appointment to do so if possible.

6. **Say,** "May I tell you a little bit about my spiritual journey?" *In a brief period—no more than three or four minutes—tell a bit about your own spiritual growth and what the Shepherd Group has meant to you.* Then say, "We're all on a spiritual journey. Would you like to share a little bit about yours with us?" Determine from this response how best to go about inviting this person or family to visit your Shepherd Group, or what activity you might share with them within the next week or two.

7. **The decision to invite them** to your Shepherd Group must be made at this time. Are they open to visiting it? Do they need more "one on one" time with you before you invite them? Or, are their problems so severe that they would disrupt the group by overtalking, seeking to dominate it, etc.? (In such cases, they may need ministering to by your Zone Pastor for a while before they enter group life.)

   What does the Spirit say to you about this person or family? Were they receptive when you brought up spiritual things, or did you sense a coldness, a lethargy, in their response? If they seemed to be thirsty for spiritual growth, they will desire to come to your group. If they are not, they may make *excuses* if asked to come—and a gap of embarrassment will be created between you by your pressing them to do something they do not desire.

8. **Some who are visited** for the first time will be unbelievers who *think* they are Christians, even though they have never made a personal commitment to Christ. Your first visit to such persons will not be your *last* visit. Keep the relationship open! Continue to cultivate your friendship with them. Your primary task is not to get them to attend the Shepherd Group the next time it meets—it's to *bring to them the life of the Lord Jesus.* Don't leave them with the impression that you are nothing more than a "Shepherd Group Salesperson!"

9. **Always, *always* close in prayer.** Intercede for all problems which have been shared. If there is a special area of need, pray for God's power to be manifested in meeting that need. Then, after you have

left the home, jot down a list of needs you discerned. Begin to pray for this home *daily,* keeping in touch by telephone to see how the person or family are getting along.

How do you feel about making your first visit? Record those feelings in this space. Share what you write with your Equipper when you meet:

_____

_____

_____

_____

Shepherd Groups grow as a result of people being brought to Christ. Focus on *knowing Christ,* and speak only of Him until an unbeliever makes a personal commitment. You should never, *ever* make a visit "on behalf of your Shepherd Group," or even your cell group church.

Visit on behalf of your living Lord! Remember this statement in Acts 2:47: *"And day by day **the Lord** added to their number **those whom He was saving."*** You don't have to be *successful*—just *faithful!*

PRACTICAL ASSIGNMENT

Your weekly Practical Assignment is the very *heart* of this course! Do not consider it an "optional" activity. Each project assigned will help you mature as a Christian and make you an effective servant of your Lord. Be faithful in completing each task. Eleven weeks from now, you'll be glad you did!

THIS WEEK...

1. Memorize Matthew 28:18-20.

2. Read the scriptures printed in this chapter each day this week.

3. Make at least one visit with your Equipper, observing him/her and the rapport established with those visited. Learn from this experience. Consider the parts of the visit you felt you could repeat what you observed your partner doing, and other parts where you may have felt inadequate, perhaps unskilled. Discuss these together after the visit.

4. Pray daily for those you met while visiting. You'll quickly discover you care far more for those you are praying for than for those you don't pray for!

(Note: Your study must be done in conjunction with DOING as well as LEARNING. Make at least one visit with your Equipper after reviewing this chapter. Don't move on to the next Unit until after you have done so!)

Insights

Jot down topics you
wish to discuss with
your Equipper:

UNIT TWO
OUR MESSAGE:
PART 1

TRUTHS YOU WILL WANT TO SHARE

In this Unit, we will discuss your message to unbelievers. In the next Unit, we will review your message to believers.

Before examining your message, it will be helpful for you to contrast the ministries of the VISITING TEAMS and SHARE GROUP TEAMS within your Shepherd Group:

VISITING TEAMS AND SHARE GROUP TEAMS COMPARED	
VISITING TEAMS	**SHARE GROUP TEAMS**
Two to a team	**Three to a team**
Reaches out to those who visit functions of the cell church (Celebrations, Congregations).	Makes contact with those who have no interest in attending any type of religious service.
Touches unbelievers who have a basic understanding of the Christian message.	**Touches unbelievers who often have no understanding of the Christian message.**
Makes contact with Christians who are needing fellowship, nurture, and equipping for ministry.	Makes contact with no Christians at all, except those who may be bitter, disillusioned, and wary of church life.
Harvest is frequently easy and response is seen quickly.	**Harvest is frequently difficult and response takes a long time.**

Why do you think your experiences as a visitor for your Shepherd Group will equip you for a later time when you will become a part of a Share Group Team?

☐ **It's easier to reach searching than stubborn hearts.**

☐ **Learning how to share my faith with the responsive people prepares me for the tougher tasks.**

☐ **Both of the above.**

☐ **Neither of the above.**

TWO TYPES OF UNBELIEVERS

That's right—two types! Later, we'll subdivide them again into three stages of "Type A's" and two stages of "Type B's." First, let's learn about "A" and "B" types...

TYPE A UNBELIEVERS: THE "LIKE US" PEOPLE, EASILY REACHED

1. They have attended a Celebration or Congregation meeting, and have been referred to you because they signed a visitor's card.

2. They already believe in God, accept the Bible, understand that Jesus is the Son of God, and have some awareness of scripture facts (like Christ's death on the cross).

3. They may already have a church membership somewhere, but are inactive—perhaps have been so for years.

4. They are searching for something, and have come to our congregation in their search.

5. They may not have all the "pieces of the puzzle" in place as far as Christian knowledge is concerned.

6. Bible Study, and explaining the plan of Salvation, are appropriate activities to share with them.

...THESE PEOPLE ARE REACHED THROUGH VISITATION!

TYPE B UNBELIEVERS: "HIDDEN" PEOPLE, NEEDING CULTIVATION

1. They seldom attend church; have no desire to do so.

2. They may not believe in God, do not accept the Bible, do not understand Jesus is the Son of God, and have very little awareness of scripture truths.

3. They have no active church membership.

4. They are not searching for the Lord's purpose for their lives, and have no intention of visiting church activities.

5. They have very few of the "pieces of the puzzle" in place as far as Christian knowledge is concerned.

6. Bible Study or discussing the plan of Salvation aren't appropriate activities to do with them at the start. *There must first be a time of developing relationships*—exposing them to the reality of the living Christ in our own lives.

...THESE PEOPLE ARE REACHED THROUGH SHARE GROUPS!

THIS PYRAMID FURTHER EXPLAINS TYPE "A" AND TYPE "B" PERSONS

In months to come, you will want to "graduate" from ministering to type "A" to type "B" unbelievers. When that time comes, your first step will be to attend the special training sessions which will be provided to equip you for this new ministry.

TYPE **"A"**

COMMITMENT

TYPE **"B"**

BIBLE STUDY

SHARE GROUP

Open To **MESSAGE**

Open To **MESSENGER**

AWARE, BUT NOT RECEPTIVE

Two Problems: DOES or DOESN'T know a Christian

NO AWARENESS OF THE GOSPEL

"Baptist or Buddhist—different roads to the same place!"

Why will it be important for you to learn to share your faith with "Type A" unbelievers before seeking to minister to "Type B" unbelievers?

(CHECK ALL ANSWERS YOU ACCEPT AS TRUE:)

☐ I can expect them to understand Bible truths.

☐ I need to begin ministering to those who are most responsive, as I learn how to harvest the lost.

☐ I don't have to pray as earnestly or as long for the "Type A" unbeliever as I would need to pray for the "Type B" person.

☐ Letting the Lord use me at this level is a way of learning how He can work through my life.

"PROPER RATIONS AT THE PROPER TIME"

And the Lord said, "Who then is the faithful and sensible steward, whom his master will put in charge of his servants, to give them their rations at the proper time?"
• Luke 12:42

"Proper rations at the proper time!"—an important truth for you to remember. If someone is responsive to BIBLE STUDY, that's the ration you will want to provide. Others will be ready to make a COMMITMENT. In that case, you will want to help them pray to receive Christ. These are the two "rations" you will learn to use at this level of ministry. When you complete the Units in KNOCKING ON DOORS, OPENING HEARTS, you will be able to minister at both levels.

Should you visit persons who are not open to your visit, they will need different "rations." They are at one of the stages in "Level B." Most of the time, there must be a period of cultivation and patient relating to their needs and interests before they will be ready for BIBLE STUDY and to make a COMMITMENT. You may wish to refer them to the Share Group team for this special ministry period. In such cases, personally arrange an introduction for one of the team members, sharing your own insights about the situation. You may even wish to attend the first couple of Share Group sessions with your Equipper, being sure the relationship is bonded with the Christians who make up that team.

The differences between the two "Type A" classes of unbelievers include the following:
(CHECK ALL ANSWERS YOU ACCEPT AS TRUE:)

☐ **The difference between these two types of believers is their prior knowledge of Christian truth.**

☐ **Those who are ready for COMMITMENT will have all the "basics" in place, and are ready to be harvested.**

☐ **Those who do not have these "basics" should be helped by providing a BIBLE STUDY for them.**

(Note: discuss any questions you have about these differences with your Equipper when you next meet together.)

In later Units of your training, we'll discuss the methods for sharing at these two levels. Just now, let's concentrate on the *message* we are to share. The "Gospel" is not getting people to join a Shepherd group, but rather helping them develop a personal relationship with the living Lord. Thus, whether it's at the level of COMMITMENT or BIBLE STUDY, our goal is to introduce Jesus Christ to our new friends.

"PROPER RATIONS:" THE BIBLE STUDY LEVEL

Remember—conducting a Bible Study with a searching unbeliever must meet special needs, totally different from the needs of Christians! Our cell group church provides you with a special edition of the New Testament, entitled THE WAY HOME, for use with unbelievers.

TRUTHS COVERED IN *"THE WAY HOME"*

By familiarizing yourself with these eleven Units, you will have a grasp of the details you'll cover with an unbeliever who does not have a good grasp of the Christian message. If you, yourself, have never completed these studies, take time to do so now. Don't just read through the materials—*actually do them yourself.* You will find it much easier to guide a seeker through the sessions if you have experienced their impact in your own life!

OUTLINE OF THE WAY HOME STUDY GUIDE

STUDY GUIDE ONE: FACT OR FICTION?
The inspiration of the Bible is clearly demonstrated.

STUDY GUIDE TWO: WHAT MAKES ME TICK?
The values which control our life styles are examined.
Those of the Christian life and the unbeliever's life are contrasted.

STUDY GUIDE THREE: WHY ARE WE HERE?
Frequently, this is the greatest question in the mind of an unbeliever.

STUDY GUIDE FOUR: AHA! THE DIFFERENCE IS...
True Christian faith is contrasted with false ones; SIN and GRACE are defined.

STUDY GUIDE FIVE: WHY DO WE NEED COMMANDMENTS?
The purpose of the Ten Commandments is clarified.

STUDY GUIDE SIX: WAS JESUS A HYPOCRITE?
The deity of Christ is clearly presented.

STUDY GUIDE SEVEN: GOD IS NOT SILENT
The way God has revealed Himself is reviewed.

**STUDY GUIDE EIGHT: HOW TO BE PRACTICAL
IN AN IMPRACTICAL WORLD**
Christian Standards are described as practical, not a burden to the believer.

STUDY GUIDE NINE: MY RESPONSIBILITIES
The problem of evil is discussed.

STUDY GUIDE TEN: THAT PRECIOUS BLOOD
The reason Jesus died on the cross is presented.

STUDY GUIDE ELEVEN: THE NEW LIFE AND THE NEW LIFE STYLE
A decision for Christ is called for in this final section.

DECISION PAGE
The four steps to follow in becoming a Christian are outlined.

What impacted you the most as you reviewed the Units in The Way Home New Testament? (Share these reflections with your Equipper during your next meeting.)

_____

_____

_____

PROPER RATIONS: THE COMMITMENT LEVEL

When a person is ready to accept Christ, the Holy Spirit is obviously calling; and your friend is truly searching. In Acts 10, Cornelius is described as such a person. What did he need? Only one thing—someone to explain how he could become a child of God! Read the "proper rations" Peter gave to this Roman Gentile:

You know of Jesus of Nazareth, how God anointed Him with the Holy Spirit and with power, and how He went about doing good, and healing all who were oppressed by the devil; for God was with Him. And we are witnesses of all the things He did both in the land of the Jews and in Jerusalem. And they also put Him to death by hanging Him on a cross. God raised Him up on the third day, and granted that He should become visible, not to all the people, but to witnesses who were chosen beforehand by God, that is, to us, who ate and drank with Him after He arose from the dead. And He ordered us to preach to the people, and solemnly to testify that this is the One who has been appointed by God as Judge of the living and the dead. Of Him all the prophets bear witness that through His name every one who believes in Him has received forgiveness of sins. • *Acts 10:38-43*

When you find a "Type A" unbeliever, you need only explain how to become a believer; it's up to the Holy Spirit to do the rest. A person taking this training said, "I never realized before that most 'Type A' people are simply waiting for someone to invite them to accept Christ!"

Check the truths shared in this passage of scripture, given by Peter to Cornelius:

☐ The fact that Jesus was truly God.

☐ Jesus' sinless life, and His power.

☐ Jesus' death on the cross

☐ His resurrection from the dead.

☐ The coming judgment.

☐ All who fully entrust their lives to Him have received forgiveness of sins.

A TRUE STORY...

The little fellow was playing among his mother's special rose bushes, which had just started to produce buds. He took a scissors and cut each bud from the top, down into the blossom. When his mother discovered what he had done, she was furious! As she scolded him, big tears welled up in his eyes. He said, "Mummy, I'm sorry! I was just trying to help God make His roses bloom!"

Avoid putting pressure on a person who seems to be at the level of commitment. You may make the dreadful mistake of the little boy, if you do! *God doesn't need you to "make His roses bloom."* In His own time, in His own way, He draws men to Himself. Simply be His obedient servant in the process, and learn how to follow His leading when helping someone come to the cross.

PRACTICAL ASSIGNMENT

TAKE A MOMENT TO THINK ABOUT THE PEOPLE YOU KNOW...

From them, select an unbeliever who "fits" each category of the Pyramid you have just studied. List their names below.

TYPE "A" UNBELIEVERS

COMMITMENT: _____

BIBLE STUDY: _____

TYPE "B" UNBELIEVERS

SHARE GROUP: _____

AWARE, NOT RECEPTIVE: _____

NO AWARENESS: _____

Discuss with your Equipper why those at "Type A" levels are more appropriately *visited,* and why those at "Type B" levels will need a lot of *cultivation* before they will be ready to accept Christ as Lord.

THIS WEEK...

- Memorize Romans 10:9-10.
- Make at least one, preferably more, visits with your Equipper.

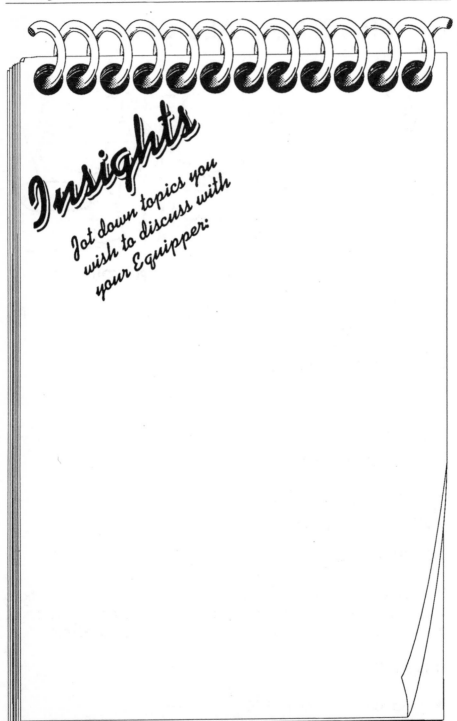

Insights

Jot down topics you wish to discuss with your Equipper:

UNIT THREE
OUR MESSAGE:
PART 2

In this Unit, we will cover the truths you will share with *believers*. Underline all the scripture passages given in this lesson in your Bible; you will use them when visiting.

Fellow Christians you visit will fall into five categories. Each category has a different need which needs to be addressed. If you familiarize yourself with the materials which follow, you'll be prepared for most of the discussions you'll have when visiting with believers.

1.   THE MEANING OF CHURCH LIFE

Does this person understand the meaning of church life? Many have never been told that it is...

A.   *A SPECIAL CALLING BY THE HOLY SPIRIT*
   * We're added to the church by the Holy Spirit: 1 Corinthians 12:12-13.
   * "Church" is literally "called out ones" in the Greek text.
   * We who are called out are "one body."
   * Together, we compose Christ's body: I Corinthians 12:27.
   * In the New Testament, the church met in small cells which moved from house to house: Acts 2:42-47.
   * We are a "cell church." Formal membership means direct participation in a Shepherd Group, for us the "basic Christian Community."

B.   *TWO PURPOSES OF CHURCH LIFE: NURTURE AND MINISTRY*
   * Nurture: I Corinthians 14:26-27. We build up one another.
   * Ministry: Ephesians 4:11-13. We are the body of Christ. If He lives through us, we will always reach the unreached!
   * Our life together calls us to be responsible *to* each other.
   * Our life together calls us to be accountable *for* each other.

What were your first questions and problems when these truths were shared with you? List the two most important ones in this space:

1. _____

2. _____

What were the answers God gave you to these two problems? List them in this space:

1. _____

2. _____

Remember these things. You may wish to share them in the conversations you will have with Christians who are hearing these truths for the first time.

2. TWO WAYS BELIEVERS WALK BEFORE GOD

Is there an inner spiritual battle going on inside this person? Find out as you share. Many believers have never been told about living...

A. AS A "CARNAL" CHRISTIAN
- Romans 7:19-24 describes the conflict.
- One throne, two "masters" demanding throne rights.
- God never intended for us to live this way!
- Romans 12:1-2: the issue can be settled!

B. AS A "SPIRITUAL" CHRISTIAN
- A deliberate choice is made: "Father, I choose your will in the place of my will in every situation I face!"
- Romans 8:12-17 describes the victory.

C. AS A "SPIRIT-FILLED" BELIEVER
- John 7:37-38: Being filled with the Spirit is not a one-time event; instead, it's a continuous activity!

- If we are not being continually filled, we are being continually emptied of His power and joy!
- Sharing our faith is the overflow of being filled with the Spirit.

How long ago did these truths impact your life? What difference was there in your daily walk when you stepped into them? Jot down these differences in the space below. Review what you write with your Equipper. Use these thoughts when visiting; there will be moments when nothing else will be quite as appropriate!

_____

_____

_____

_____

_____

3. WALKING THROUGH DEEP VALLEYS

Is this person undergoing a heavy personal crisis? Many have never been told that...

A. *GOD DOES NOT "CAUSE" SORROW, HEARTACHE!*
It's a part of sin's curse upon us. God grieves along with us that we must face these tragic circumstances!
- Sin's pain explained: Romans 8:21-23.
- The "Comforter" promised: John 14:16-18.

B. *ONE OF THE GIFTS GOD GIVES US FOR WALKING THROUGH OUR VALLEY IS FELLOWSHIP WITH OTHER CHRISTIANS.*
- This ministry explained: Galatians 6:2.
- Our life style described: Romans 15:1-2.
- The three patterns for our fellowship are given—build up, stimulate, encourage: I Corinthians 14:3.

31

4. ALL CHRISTIANS ARE MINISTERS

Is the person you are visiting aware that *all Christians* are called to minister to others? Many have never been told about...

A. THE TWO "WORLDS" OF THE BELIEVER...

THE NATURAL WORLD FOR NATURAL PERSONS

I CORINTHIANS 2:14: "A man who is unspiritual refuses what belongs to the Spirit of God..."

SELF-CENTERED
HEARS NATURAL SOUNDS
SEES PHYSICAL OBJECTS
FILLED WITH PRIDE
SMELLS NATURAL ODORS
LOVES WITH HUMAN LOVE

MANY TALENTS

SKILLS
ABILITIES
STRENGTHS

THE SPIRITUAL WORLD FOR SPIRITUAL PERSONS

I CORINTHIANS 2:15: "A man gifted with the Spirit can judge the worth of everything..."

IS FILLED WITH COMPASSION
HEARS SPIRITUAL SOUNDS
SEES SPIRITUAL TRUTHS
HAS SPIRITUAL BOLDNESS
SENSES THINGS OF THE SPIRIT
LOVES WITH CHRIST'S LOVE

MANY GIFTS

SERVING
GIVING   DISCERNING
FAITH   TRUE/FALSE
PROPHECY   SPIRITS
WISE   TEACHING
  SPEECH   ETC.

Since Christ came to live in your life, "all things have become new." You have entered the spiritual world, and you see things in a new way. Can you list four areas in your life that have dramatically changed? These areas might become a part of your testimony as you visit with an unbeliever, or with an immature Christian you visit. List four such areas below:

1.＿＿＿＿＿＿＿＿＿＿＿＿＿＿＿＿＿＿＿＿＿＿＿＿

2.＿＿＿＿＿＿＿＿＿＿＿＿＿＿＿＿＿＿＿＿＿＿＿＿

3.＿＿＿＿＿＿＿＿＿＿＿＿＿＿＿＿＿＿＿＿＿＿＿＿

4.＿＿＿＿＿＿＿＿＿＿＿＿＿＿＿＿＿＿＿＿＿＿＿＿

B. THE "SPIRITUAL TOOLS" WE ARE GIVEN...

We can use our TALENTS for the Lord, but when He assigns us a SPIRITUAL TASK, we must use His SPIRITUAL GIFTS, or "tools," which are required to accomplish His work.

- Detailed explanation is given in I Corinthians 12 and Romans 12.
- Share with the person you are visiting, "As you enter our Shepherd Group, we'll seek to help you discover and use your spiritual gifts. They alone will reveal the work of God through your life."

Check the needs below that can only be met as you exercise spiritual gifts:

☐ **Prayer for the healing of a person who is ill.**

☐ **Helping a person clean his home.**

☐ **Discerning spiritual needs in the life of another.**

☐ **Giving a person money to help with the bills.**

C. THE SPECIAL ASSIGNMENT FOR EACH ONE OF US...

- Every single, solitary believer is a minister: I Peter 2:9-10.
- Our pastoral leadership is responsible to equip us for our ministry: Ephesians 4:11-12.
- Therefore, we look to our pastoral leadership for guidance, but we do not expect them to perform *our* ministries!

If only the pastoral team were to visit our visitors, what would be the negative results? Answer below:

_____

_____

_____

_____

33

5. SOME TRUTHS THAT ARE PRECIOUS TO US

We believe the Bible, both Old and New Testaments, are our guide in all matters of faith and practice. Therefore, we believe *all* that the Bible teaches. However, there are some truths which we believe are particularly relevant to our life together. Other Christian communities believe some or all of the truths shared below; the *literal application of them* is what has richly blessed our lives.

A. THE LORDSHIP OF CHRIST

All of our distinctive principles may be said to grow out of one great truth: the absolute Lordship of Christ. In our Shepherd Group, we constantly ask ourselves,
- "What did our Lord Jesus say about life situations?"
- "What did he do?"
- "What does He want us to do?"

As we answer these questions honestly, we discover it gives us direction in every area of our personal life.

Check the boxes which describe the life of a Christian who has *not* accepted the Lordship of Christ:

☐ **Accepts a new job without praying about it first.**

☐ **Is willing to do God's will, regardless of the cost.**

☐ **Avoids ministries interfering with personal plans.**

☐ **Primary goal is becoming successful in life.**

☐ **Truly enjoys ministering, and receiving ministry.**

☐ **Has no prayer life, no interest in personal Bible study.**

A TRUE STORY...

A Chinese Christian boarded a train and entered the compartment assigned to him for the long ride to Canton. The other man assigned to the compartment took out a deck of cards and a bottle of whiskey. "We shall have a long trip," he said. "Let's drink and gamble to pass

34

the time!" The Christian said, "I must apologize. I cannot play and drink with you, for I don't have my hands with me any more." The unbeliever was perplexed, for the Christian's hands were clearly visible. "I see you don't understand. These *used* to be my hands until I met Jesus. When they were my hands, they often gambled and drank whiskey. But Christ asked me to give Him my body as well as my mind and my desires. I did so—and since then, He has owned my hands. Not once since He has owned them have I felt Him desiring to drink or gamble. I don't mean to offend you, but I can't play. I don't have my hands with me."

B. THE AUTHORITY AND SUFFICIENCY OF THE BIBLE

ONLY ONE BOOK IS INSPIRED BY GOD!

For us, the New Testament is the rule of faith and practice. By it all creeds, principles, programs, and practices are to be judged. When any question of doctrine or practice arises, we ask only one question: *"What does the scripture say?"* (Romans 4:3).

Read Revelation 22:18-19; then check the books below that we can accept as also inspired by God as is the Bible:

☐ **The Book of Mormon.**

☐ **Any writings of non-Christian religions.**

☐ **Both of the above.**

☐ **Neither of the above.**

C. THE COMPETENCY OF THE INDIVIDUAL BEFORE GOD

We believe that every individual has the right to approach God for himself and that no person, institution, or ordinance should come between the soul and God. Each individual must hear, heed, repent, believe, be baptized, worship, contribute, and serve the Lord as a *personal* commitment.

D. A CONVERTED CHURCH

Only persons who are old enough to make an intelligent choice, to realize and repent of sin, and to accept Christ as a definite and voluntary act of faith become a part of our church. We seek to bring our own children to make that choice for themselves. We also seek to share the good news that Christ has called *all persons* to follow Him, and to lead many to commit their lives to Him.

E. CHURCH LIFE IS MADE UP OF "BASIC CHRISTIAN COMMUNITIES"

In Acts 2:42-46, we discover the New Testament church created home cell groups as their very first pattern for meeting together. We have realized that true fellowship and "building up one another" is *never done effectively* unless church life begins with "spiritual families." Becoming a part of our church means becoming a part of a Shepherd Group—that's what we call our "Basic Christian Community."

Most probably the person you are visiting has never heard of a "cell group church" made up of "Shepherd groups." As you seek to explain it, which of the following approaches would be most appropriate to use?

☐ **Read Acts 2:42-46. Explain they are scriptural.**

☐ **Share your testimony about your experience in one.**

☐ **Use both of the above to explain Shepherd groups.**

☐ **Do you have a better idea? If so, jot it down here:**

F. ALL THE SHEPHERD GROUPS GATHER FOR "CELEBRATIONS"

Worship by the entire body of Christ is a powerful and necessary experience. Our "Celebrations" focus on praise and worship, prayer, and the clear teaching of scripture. We don't consider a Celebration a *church service;* rather, it's an *event* of Shepherd group life in which we all rejoice together and prostrate ourselves before the Lord. It may last two hours; sometimes even longer, because it *is* an event, and not just a church service. We love being together and sharing our common life in this manner. No Shepherd group is independent of the rest of the body of Christ, but is always under the guidance of our pastors. Our vision is to develop hundreds of Shepherd groups, with all of them gathering for our Celebrations.

One of the concerns of a "cell group church" is the danger of collecting people who attend only the Celebrations, and who never enter into the true life and ministry of the church. Such uncommitted people can dilute the work of the Spirit by selfishly using our public meetings for personal gratification. Which of the following comments "fits" you in explaining this to those you visit?

☐ **"The true life of our body is not in our Celebrations, but in our living together in the personal relationships of a Shepherd group. You owe it to yourself to visit our group, and discover for yourself what I'm talking about. There's no obligation."**

☐ **"I'd like to encourage you to discover the *true church* we share together—our Shepherd groups. Would you permit me to pick you up and take you to our next one? I think you will be overwhelmed by what you discover there!"**

☐ **"We often miss the reality of the Christian life by only attending large, impersonal gatherings. The growth of our spiritual lives requires us to be a part of a small group, where we can become committed in love to others. I never grew in my ministry until I became a part of a Shepherd group. May I pick you up and take you to our next one?"**

G. WE SHARE TWO ORDINANCES TOGETHER

We believe that Baptism and the Lord's Supper are *Ordinances,* rather than *Sacraments.* That is, they are symbols. They do not bring salvation, nor do they impart forgiveness of sin. However, they are precious to us and bring a great spiritual blessing to all who participate in them.

H. BAPTISM IS RESERVED FOR BELIEVERS

We believe that only those persons who have repented (turned away) from their sins and who have received Jesus Christ as Savior and Lord are proper subjects for baptism. It's a time of great celebration when this public witness of conversion is given.

In the book of Acts, baptism was performed by men who were not officials of a formal church (Acts 8:26-40). Of course, those who serve as our pastors are always glad to perform this ordinance. We often encourage our members who have won a friend or relative to Christ to be the one who performs the baptism, and will gladly give instructions for doing so. It's particularly beautiful to see a Christian father baptizing his own son or daughter. It's a part of our conviction that we are *all ministers,* and that the division between "clergy" and "laymen" is totally unscriptural and man-made. However, such baptisms are to be affirmed *in advance* by the pastoral staff, to insure the meaning of baptism and the commitment of the person's conversion are real.

Read the story of Philip and the Ethiopian eunuch in Acts 8:26-39. Which of the following comments are true about this meeting?

- [ ] **Philip was not an "ordained minister" of a church.**
- [ ] **The eunuch first received Christ before being baptized.**
- [ ] **There was a waiting period for the eunuch to prove he was truly converted before he was baptized.**
- [ ] **God knew the eunuch wanted to follow Him, and sent Philip to meet him by the roadside.**

I. THE LORD'S SUPPER REMINDS US OF CALVARY, WHERE WE RECEIVED ETERNAL LIFE AND WERE ADDED TO THE BODY OF CHRIST.

At the cross, our Lord shed His blood and allowed His body to be broken for us. He Himself told His disciples to observe the ordinance "in remembrance of Him." No more important event has ever taken place in all of history! The sharing of this event is most precious to us. We treasure the times we observe it.

Through the centuries, the *true meaning* of the Lord's Supper was grossly distorted by the church. It has been taught for centuries that the bread actually turns into the flesh of Christ when it enters the body, cleansing the person of sin. This is not taught anywhere in scripture. Rather, Jesus taught the ordinance was a *remembrance*—nothing more. Our cleansing took place at Calvary. John tells us it is the blood of Jesus Christ that cleanses us from all sin (I John 1:7). The Lord's Supper is a remembrance of this.

But—there's more! Do you recall how God took Adam's bride from his side? Paul tells us in Romans 5:14 that Christ is the "second Adam." Where and when was the church, the Bride of Christ, born? *At the cross*—as the side of our Lord was pierced—as blood and water flowed from His wound. By His death, He gave birth to His bride. Thus, it's most fitting that we remember how *our* new birth, and the birth of the *church*, both came from His substitutionary death. In I Corinthians 10:16-17, we are reminded that the Lord's Supper is the "communion of the body of Christ." In I Corinthians 11:29-30, we are clearly told that partaking of the bread and the wine without "discerning the body" causes many to be "weak and sickly, and many sleep."

In the first century, the Lord's Supper was regularly conducted in the homes of Christians, attached to the *"Love Feasts"* of their home meetings. We recognize this ordinance can be celebrated in more public settings, but we *particularly* cherish observing it together in some of our Shepherd Group meetings, accompanied by a meal we call *our* "Love Feast." It's something all Christians should experience.

Under what circumstances would you discuss the meaning of the Lord's Supper when making a visit?
(Check your choices)

☐ In discussing the meaning of the crucifixion.

☐ In replying to direct questions about it.

☐ When inviting a person to your group when you know the ordinance will be observed.

☐ As a means of sharing the full meaning of the death of Christ, and His purpose for allowing Himself to be crucified.

PRACTICAL ASSIGNMENT

INSIGHTS...

Discuss with your Equipper the two "worlds" of the believer, as illustrated in this Unit. How aware have you been of these two "worlds?" What can you do or say when visiting which will help those you serve to understand this truth? *Do you fully understand what you have learned?* If you do, you will be a blessing to those who hear these things for the first time.

THIS WEEK...

• Make at least one visit with your Equipper.

• Mark all the scripture verses given in this week's material. You may also wish to create an "index" on a front fly page of your Bible to know where to turn to find scriptures dealing with a certain person's need. Have you marked *this* verse yet?

Call unto me and I will answer thee and show thee great and mighty things which thou knowest not.
• *Jeremiah 33:3*

Insights

Jot down topics you wish to discuss with your Equipper:

UNIT FOUR
OUR VISITATION
METHODS—I

WHY USE THE TELEPHONE FOR VISITING VISITORS?

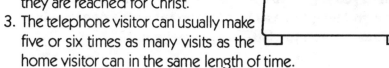

1. Telephone visits can help cultivate the unchurched people for meaningful home visits later.
2. It is the only way the typical Shepherd Group can keep in touch with every visitor, every month, until they are reached for Christ.
3. The telephone visitor can usually make five or six times as many visits as the home visitor can in the same length of time.
4. All Shepherd Group workers can make telephone visits. Everyone can be involved in this outreach ministry!
5. The telephone ministry is not hindered by transportation problems, baby-sitting problems, physical disabilities, bad weather, unfamiliar streets in strange areas, etc.
6. Your telephone conversations will help you "grade" your contacts and gather needed information to make a more effective visit later.
7. A consistent telephone ministry will help you maintain an accurate, up-to-date record of people who need to be reached.
8. The "Love Lines" of communication will always be *UP* between you and the visitor to your cell group public services.

When is it appropriate to make telephone calls related to visiting people?

☐ **Before scheduling your first visit.**

☐ **Before 9:30 a.m. or after 8:30 p.m.**

☐ **As a follow-up to a visit, a way of keeping in touch.**

☐ **As a substitute for a visit you ought to make.**

WHO WILL YOU BE CALLING?

1. Some may have visited in a worship service; others will have attended one of our special public events.
2. Visitors assigned to you—people who will often have serious spiritual or physical needs.
3. Some may be deeply interested in becoming a part of your Shepherd group.
4. Some may be inactive members of other local churches.
5. Some may be only slightly interested in our fellowship, or have little or no interest in returning to visit us.

Should you regard the person who doesn't seem to be friendly when you telephone as less important as the one who is very anxious for you to visit? Why, or why not?

_____

_____

_____

THE PURPOSE OF YOUR TELEPHONE CALLS

1. Ultimately, to bring each person to know Christ and the abundant life, Christian discipleship, and become an active member of your Shepherd group.
2. Another key objective: get a commitment to let you make a visit. Offer to come at a time convenient to the family.

3. To get acquainted with them, and to acquaint them with your Shepherd group, as well as the ministries of our cell group church.
4. To build a bridge of friendship between the person and your Shepherd Group.
5. To invite them to attend your Shepherd group and/or a Worship Service.
6. To offer any assistance you and the Shepherd group can provide.
7. To prepare the way for other members of your Shepherd group to make other meaningful visits in the home at a later date.

A TRUE STORY...

She was so depressed she felt she might try to take her life. She got dressed and made her way to a Celebration of a cell group church. She deliberately slipped in late and left a few minutes before the service ended, so she wouldn't have to speak to anyone. However, she *had* filled out a visitor's card. The Shepherd group person who called was very sensitive, very caring, and drew this information out of her. She prayed with her over the telephone. At the close of the call, the woman said, "You'll never know how much your call has meant to me!"

In the story above, what might have been the outcome if the person calling was concerned only about making an appointment to visit this woman? Would she have felt she was being "used" by a religous group who didn't care about her needs? Explain your answer:

_____

_____

WHEN TO MAKE TELEPHONE CALLS TO PEOPLE

1. Be sure to choose the time *most convenient* for you and the people you are calling.
2. Saturdays are best—especially during the mornings.
3. Week nights are usually good. Weekday mornings are effective for those who do not work.

4. Select a time when most families are not engaged in activities such as working, eating, sleeping, etc.
5. If the telephone number given is a place of business, call briefly during office hours. Get a home phone number.

BEFORE YOU DIAL

1. Pray that God will guide you in this effort, and seek His leadership for your effort.
2. Be as familiar with the facts about the family/person as possible! But—you can call effectively *without* any facts by being sensitive and carefully listening to the *mood* of the person as well as the words.
3. If the name of the person is not familiar to you and hard to pronounce, make your best attempt! Ask the person to pronounce the name for you—and say it aloud. Write the correct pronunciation on the visitation card.

"Pray before you call!" What difference will it make when you talk to the Lord about each call just before it is made?
(Check answers you consider to be correct)

☐ **The empowering of the Spirit will be in your voice.**

☐ **It assures you that everyone will invite you to visit.**

☐ **Christ's love will flow through you in a special way.**

☐ **The presence of the Lord will be present in the call.**

THE TELEPHONE CONVERSATION

1. Be kind and Christlike in all situations. We are to win friends for Him and His body.
2. Your attitude and approach is critical.
3. Your Visitation Card will reveal most of the information our cell group church has about the family/person. Sometimes the available information is not as complete as is desirable. Part of it may be inaccurate or misleading.
4. You may need to obtain some additional information during the conversation to complete or correct the information on the card.

5. In some cases, the family may have decided to become active in another church. Express joy for this, and encourage them to be active in their new church. Remind them that they are welcome to visit our church at any time.

6. Some may say that they are attending another church but still are undecided about membership. Invite them to visit your Shepherd group before making their decision.

7. Speak clearly and distinctly into the telephone.

8. Be casual and informal during the phone call. The attitude and disposition of the person with whom you are talking will help determine the length of the conversation and the nature of the discussion. *Be brief*—but take enough time to accomplish your purpose. Usually a short conversation is best, but don't rush it...or let it drag!

9. Don't get involved in a debate. You don't have to prove anything.

YOUR CONVERSATION MAY GO SOMETHING LIKE THIS...

"Hello, is this Mr. (Mrs.)_____? (Or, use first name)

"I am from (name of our cell group church). I just wanted to get acquainted with you by phone. Is this a convenient time for you?"

OR..."I have been wanting to meet you and thank you for visiting our fellowship..."

OR..."We were glad to have you attend our worship services (Sunday, recently)..."

Earlier in your training, we suggested you focus on representing our Lord Jesus Christ first of all, not your church or your Shepherd Group. At this point in the material, jot down your feelings about this suggestion. Share them with your Equipper:

_____

_____

_____

DURING THE CONVERSATION YOU COULD DISCUSS...

1. Share your testimony: your conversion, etc.
2. Their personal response to the worship and the message in the service they attended. *Probe for their spiritual need!*
3. When, and where, have they had real encounters with Christ in the past?
4. Seek to draw out any prior conversion commitment if it is appropriate to do so; if not, delay this area until you make your first visit.
5. What Christian family members or friends do they have?
6. Location and time of your Shepherd group meeting.
7. Confirm any of the information on the card if you have any doubt about it—especially the address, flat/apartment number, or location. Directions to their residence is helpful if you don't know the area where they live.
8. Before you conclude the conversation, get a commitment from them to let you visit!
9. You may pray over the phone with the person about a specific need, such as sickness, sorrow, trouble, etc.

YOU MIGHT CLOSE BY COMMENTING...

"I've enjoyed talking with you. I'm looking forward to meeting you personally very soon, etc."
OR..."I'm anxious to visit in your home, etc."

What is the difference between a "salesman for a church" and a true representative of Christ?
(Check all answers you consider to be correct)

☐ The "salesman's" interest is in getting members to join the church organization, and only secondarily in bringing people to know Christ as Lord.

☐ A true representative of Christ knows the church is an organism, not an organization. Thus, the focus will be placed on sharing the living Lord, and bringing the person to experience His love and power first of all.

☐ Both of the above are true statements.

REPORTING THE TELEPHONE VISIT

1. An accurate report of your visit may be as important as the visit itself in the long term.
2. Make your report on the form you are given to use.
3. Turn this report over to the person assigned to collect it from you right away!
4. Be honest and specific in your report and your evaluation of the visit. Write your name on the card. Indicate if a further visit is needed by the Shepherd or a pastor.

Explain in detail what this statement means:
"If you don't keep good records about your visits, you are clearly saying, 'This person is of no consequence...not even important enough for me to take the time to complete a report of my visit!' " (Discuss your answer with your Equipper.)

_____

_____

_____

THOUGHTS TO REMEMBER...

1. Some of the people you call will express a sincere, genuine interest and appreciation for your call. Others will be indifferent, with no positive response. Remember in these cases that they don't know you; they aren't rejecting you, but the issue of becoming involved in a relationship they may not be able to accept at this time.
2. Don't become discouraged. Remember that people usually will not show any interest in their own spiritual condition until we show concern for them!
3. Our part in fulfilling the Great Commission includes using the telephone to share our faith. This is one way to saturate our community with the good news about Jesus, and to tell more about the most exciting life which can be experienced: living in the body of Christ!

PRACTICAL ASSIGNMENT

INSIGHTS...

By this time, your Equipper has made phone calls in your presence. This week, you will be making them while you are observed by him/her. When you finish the first call, reflect on these two questions:

1. Did you discover whether the person was, or was not, a believer?

2. Was your call appropriate for a "Level 1" unbeliever, who came to church seeking for Christ?

THIS WEEK...

• Call one of the people you have already visited and let him know you are thinking about him. Give a word of encouragement, have a moment of prayer, etc., as seems appropriate.

• Complete the report forms after you make the first telephone calls to new people you have not yet visited.

• Review the scripture verses you have studied and underlined in your Bible since you began to take this journey into ministry.

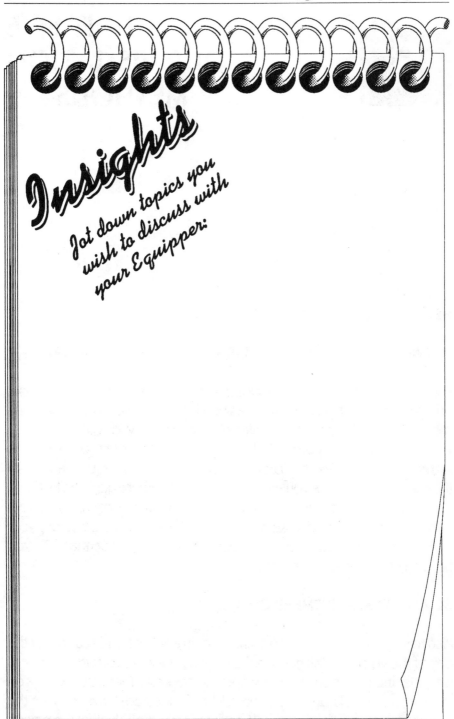

Insights

Jot down topics you wish to discuss with your Equipper:

UNIT FIVE
OUR VISITATION
METHODS—2

HELPFUL HINTS FOR THE VISITATION CALL...

1. CAREFULLY FOLLOW THE GUIDANCE OF YOUR EQUIPPER.

It is best for you to observe your Equipper for the first few visits. Next, you will be observed by him/her as you become responsible for taking the lead in the sharing. You will decide in advance who will be the "lead visitor" or "speaking partner." This person talks most; the other person prays most! If you are the "praying partner," don't interrupt the flow of the conversation unless you are asked to share by your Equipper. By being careful about this matter, you won't interrupt the flow of ministry by your partner. If it is deemed wise for you to enter into the discussion, your partner will invite you to do so by being asked by your partner, "Do you have any thoughts on this matter?"

2. VISIT BY APPOINTMENT ONLY.

Plan to visit by making your appointments in advance, preferably *not* the day of the visit. You will gain confidence by knowing you are expected. Get specific directions to easily find the address. Then, *be exactly on time.* If you don't know where the address is located, leave early for the appointment—and if you arrive 15 minutes early, *don't* bother the person until the proper time has arrived. The only thing more upsetting than someone who shows up 15 minutes late for an appointment is someone who comes 15 minutes early!

3. BRING ALONG SOMETHING YOU CAN LEAVE.

Take an invitation and map to a Shepherd group function, a tape of the Pastor's sermon, etc.

A TRUE STORY...
A Shepherd group decided to have a "Love Feast" along with their regular weekly meeting, and to do this once a month. It was agreed that each family would bring a main dish, and that the different host families would provide the beverages and the elements for the observing of the Lord's Supper. From this, they got an idea about how they could make those being visited feel welcome. All those visited the week before the "Love Feast" were given a frozen dish to heat and bring along when they attended the Shepherd group. They had such a positive response to this that they decided to do it every week, announcing as they did so the date of the next "Love Feast."

4. HAVE PRAYER BEFORE MAKING EACH VISIT.

Visitation is for the purpose of sharing the good news about Jesus Christ, showing His love and concern. Obviously, we desire that the person will become a part of our fellowship. We want the Lord to be in control of the experience. We want to be "tuned in" to what He has in mind. Bathe the visit in prayer.

5. BE COURTEOUS AND SENSITIVE.

You only get one chance to make a first impression! Avoid loud talking between yourselves while waiting for someone to answer the door. Ring the door bell or knock; then wait. If no one comes to the door, leave a note and telephone the person later. Visit with a spirit of being able to forget yourself. Have a genuine interest in your new friend. For that hour or so, he/she is the most important person in the world!

What are the benefits you are experiencing by visiting with your Equipper? Jot down some of them in this space, and share them when you next get together to visit...

_____

_____

_____

6. DURING THE VISIT...

1. Have a sense of humor! Smile when the door opens.
2. Thank the person for the privilege of visiting with him/her.
3. Look around the residence for pictures, collections, etc. What are the things which seem important to this person? Ask questions about these things. Find a common bond.
4. Always be aware of the person's tones of voice (and your own!), the interest (or lack of it) in what you are saying, and facial expressions. Is the person glad you are present? Is the person simply being polite until you leave? *Can you tell?*

7. USE GOOD MANNERS!

If you are offered something to eat, take it if at all possible. If you must decline, do so graciously—especially if you realize the person has prepared food to serve during your visit. Try not to stay too long...nor leave too quickly.

SOME QUESTIONS TO ASK...

1. How would you describe your relationship with the Lord at this time in your life? *Note:* be sensitive about how far you can pursue this on a first visit. Perhaps you can share a part of your own testimony which relates to their experiences and open the door to a discussion of their walk with the Lord.
4. As the Holy Spirit prompts you to do so, share Jesus Christ with each person who has obviously never been born again.

5. As you become comfortable in making visits, you will naturally begin to share your Christian experience and explain the way they, too, can become a Christian. (In this course, you will learn a simple way to lead a person to Christ.)

If you are the observer and your Equipper is the one doing the talking, what should you do?
(Check responses you consider to be appropriate:)

☐ **Pray under your breath for the Spirit to work.**

☐ **Listen sensitively to the undertones of the discussion.**

☐ **Chime in often; give your thoughts on each topic.**

☐ **Enter the discussion when your Equipper asks you to share your thoughts or give your testimony, etc.**

SOME FACTS WHICH MOST VISITORS FIND INTERESTING

1. We are interested in helping each person discover and use to the fullest his/her spiritual gifts. Our Shepherd group seeks to help each new member grow into a personal ministry. The Shepherd of each group arranges a personal interview with each incoming person to help with this.
2. We have had many new members in our Shepherd Groups during the past months. If they choose to join our cell group church, they will find many others who have not been "around" a long time!
3. We usually suggest newcomers visit a Shepherd Group for three or four weeks, and then attend the Spiritual Formation Weekend conducted by the leadership for those interested in being a part of our life together.

SOME THOUGHTS TO REMEMBER...

1. If questions arise which you cannot answer, or if the person needs materials you do not have with you, assure them that you will be back in touch...and do it!
2. If the situation is right, always have prayer before you leave.
3. Let the person know they can call on you if they need anything. Leave your card or phone number.

4. Accept this person as "yours" to be loved and nurtured. Minister to each need as best you can. This might require your involving another member of the Shepherd group. Don't be a "pest," but stay in touch with each person by telephone calls, visits, etc.
5. Be open to the Lord's guidance. Find your own approaches to this ministry.

List two things you have learned from your visiting since you began this training about the way people respond to the discussion of spiritual things. Share these insights with your Equipper.

1._____

2._____

HE IS NO FOOL WHO GIVES
WHAT HE CANNOT KEEP
TO GAIN WHAT HE CANNOT LOSE.

PRACTICAL ASSIGNMENT

INSIGHTS...

Remember the last two visits you and your Equipper made:

1. Did the people visited feel as though they were entertaining salesmen for your cell group church, or that they were making new friends?

2. Did the persons visited feel they *listened* more than they *talked*?

THIS WEEK...

Visit with your Equipper this week.

Enter into sharing in the visit as instructed in advance by your Equipper.

Insights

Jot down topics you wish to discuss with your Equipper:

UNIT SIX
OUR VISITATION
METHODS—3

AFTER THE CALL OR VISIT...WHAT THEN?

You take out a "contract to care" each time you call or visit a person. Your sincere interest as you make the initial contact may be the start of a lifelong relationship. Indeed, you may be meeting one of your best friends for years to come.

TWO POSITIVE RESPONSES TO YOUR VISIT

1. The person will immediately join your Shepherd group and enter into group life.

2. The person will accept Christ, be helped to understand the meaning of baptism in greater detail, and begin to grow spiritually through your Shepherd group.

IN EITHER CASE, YOU PLAY A SPECIAL ROLE!
"BONDING" IS A VITAL MINISTRY...

Many Church Growth studies have been made about the steps people make when joining a cell group church. These studies show that the critical decision to become a part of the ministry is made *after the second or third visit, not the first one.*

Why should your second and third visits mean as much, or more, than the first visit?

☐ **The second and third visits show you really care.**

☐ **The first visit establishes contact; the next two visits develop a meaningful relationship.**

☐ **Both of the above are true.**

☐ **Only one of the above statements is true.**

THINK THE WAY THE PERSON YOU'RE VISITING THINKS:

First visit to our church: "What is their worship service like? How friendly are the people? Do I feel comfortable here?"

YOUR VISIT AT THIS TIME WILL BE A RESPONSE TO THESE QUESTIONS. IF YOU ARE FRIENDLY...IF THEY FEEL COMFORTABLE WITH YOU...THEY WILL LOOK FORWARD TO ADDITIONAL CONTACTS WITH YOU.

Second visit to our worship service: "I felt good about the first visit. I wonder if I'll still feel that way if I go back again?"

THIS IS THE CRITICAL TIME! IF YOU ARE A VITAL PART OF THAT SECOND VISIT THEY MAKE TO OUR CHURCH...IF YOU REALLY CARE...IF YOU GO OUT OF YOUR WAY TO INTRODUCE THEM TO PEOPLE...IF THEY FEEL ACCEPTED...THEY WILL WANT TO VISIT YOUR SHEPHERD GROUP. A SECOND PERSONAL VISIT OR A TELEPHONE CONTACT AT THIS STAGE IS A VERY SPECIAL WAY OF SAYING, "I REALLY FEEL YOU ARE A SPECIAL PERSON !"

It will probably be at this time they will decide to visit your Shepherd group. If they are made to feel loved and welcomed into the group, they will leave with positive feelings about participating.

Third visit, hopefully to the Shepherd group as well as the public worship service: "Could I make friends here? Would I be accepted? Does the Shepherd group fit me? Would I feel comfortable bringing my friends to this church? Will my needs be met? Have they reached out to me? Do some here really care about me?"

FOR A VERY HIGH PERCENTAGE OF PEOPLE, THIS VISIT WILL BE THE DECISION-MAKING TIME. WHETHER OR NOT THEY ACTUALLY JOIN AT ONCE, THE CHOICE WILL BE SHAPED IN THEIR HEARTS. ANOTHER CONTACT, EITHER IN PERSON OR BY TELEPHONE, IS MEANINGFUL.

DO YOU NOW RECOGNIZE THE IMPORTANCE OF WHAT WE'LL CALL THE "FOUR-TOUCH" PRINCIPLE OF VISITATION?

One contact is not enough. Whether you personally make all *four* contacts, or whether it is done by several persons, a total of *four* contacts (by telephone or in person) will insure the searching heart finds a loving home.

On which visit should you determine their relationship to Christ?
(Check all boxes which seem to be correct.)

☐ **If at all possible, on the first visit.**

☐ **It's best to wait until the third visit.**

☐ **On the second visit, when we know each other better.**

☐ **At the first opening the Holy Spirit provides.**

...BUT THE BONDING MUST CONTINUE!

When the newcomer decides to join your Shepherd group, there's no guarantee they will remain unless they are made to feel a part of the life of the group. Church Growth studies show that the following steps must be accomplished *within six months of the time of joining*, or the person will become a dropout:

1. At least two close friendships are formed.
2. Invites the Shepherd group to meet in his/her dwelling.
3. Responsibility for some area of ministry or activity is assumed.

Your friendship, guidance, and assistance to this person will "bond" him into your Shepherd group. Help each person take these steps:

1. Attend SPIRITUAL FORMATION WEEKEND.
   This course is designed to help the new person share the vision of our cell group church.
2. Meet with the Shepherd privately to review the JOURNEY GUIDE.
3. Enter training at the appropriate beginning level.
4. Become active in the equipping times which compose the first segment of the Shepherd group schedule.
5. Get involved in some area of ministry.
6. Make two or three close friends within the first six months.

Let's check you against the seven areas mentioned above! Put a ✓ by the areas which now bond you to our ministry:

☐ **I have attended the SPIRITUAL FORMATION WEEKEND.**

☐ **I have met with the Shepherd privately to review the JOURNEY GUIDE.**

☐ **I have entered training at the appropriate beginning level for me.**

☐ **I have become active in the equipping times which compose the first segment of the Shepherd group schedule.**

☐ **I have become involved in this visitation ministry.**

☐ **I have made at least two or three close friends within the first six months.**

Many people are very shy, feeling they cannot enter into relationships with others until they are "invited" to do so. Other people are outgoing, making their own way very quickly into new groups. Discern which type of persons you are ministering to, and become a very special "bridge" for the shy, inviting them to activities, introducing them to others, etc.

The following page shows a sample of the VISITATION MINISTRY CHECK LIST. Duplicate this form on any copy machine as you need it.

VISITATION MINISTRY CHECK LIST

NAME	ADDRESS
HOME PHONE	BUSINESS PHONE

DIRECTIONS TO FIND THIS ADDRESS:

MINISTRY ACTIVITY	DATE
Contacted by telephone—appointment made	
Confirmation of appointment, just before visit is made	
Personal visit made	
Second personal visit made	
Invited to attend Shepherd group as my guest	
Introduced to others at Shepherd group	
Introduced to others in greater church body	
Included in an informal time with me and my friends	
I have met his/her family members	
Person has attended two or three Shepherd group meetings	
Person has attended the Spiritual Formation Weekend	
Person has made two or more close friends in our body	
Person has accepted responsibility in our Shepherd group	
Person has invited Shepherd group to meet in his/her home	
DATE I FIRST SHARED MY WITNESS	
DATE I SHARED THE PLAN OF SALVATION	
IF NOT A BELIEVER, DATE ACCEPTED CHRIST AS LORD	
DATE OF BAPTISM	
DATE OF JOURNEY GUIDE INTERVIEW WITH SHEPHERD	

PRAYER CONCERNS (CONTINUE ON BACK OF THIS FORM)

"BONDING" IN OUR SHEPHERD GROUP...

Think about the ways you have observed "bonding" taking place in your Shepherd group:

On page 60-62, a profile of how a person first observes a church is presented. You have already evaluated your own journey, using the review which follows it. How did your own experience in joining our church match, or differ, from it?

_____

_____

Share the points of the "Four Touch" principle of visitation. In your opinion, which one of the four points is most important? Underline it; discuss with your Equipper.

_____

_____

_____

_____

Can you think of any examples of people who joined our church and who did not properly bond, and who are now inactive?

☐ Yes   ☐ No

What might have been done to avoid this from happening?

_____

In your opinions, is it possible to "re-bond" inactive members?

☐ Yes   ☐ No

...Why, or why not?

_____

PRACTICAL ASSIGNMENT

THIS WEEK...

1. Make a visit with your Equipper.

2. Follow up on at least one previous contact you have made, using the Visitation Ministry Check List.

3. Pray daily for each person you have contacted thus far in your visitation ministry.

Insights

Jot down topics you wish to discuss with your Equipper:

UNIT SEVEN
HOW TO LEAD A LOST
PERSON TO CHRIST—I

A CALL TO BECOME MORE THAN A "CHURCH VISITOR!"

When you visit a "TYPE A" unbeliever, you have often come to a field ripe for harvest! Don't ever miss the opportunity to help a person pass from death to life. This Unit, and the ones which follow, will give you the basic tools to do this. First, let's talk a bit about *when* it's the proper time to lead a lost person to Christ.

If you are a brand new Christian yourself, you're probably not aware that traditional churches for the past 50 years have been practicing a pattern of winning people to Christ which uses pre-memorized presentations. These "one way presentations" were absolutely necessary, because little or no attempt was ever made to develop true bonds of love between believers and unbelievers. On the very first contact, the person was asked an opening question about their relationship to Jesus Christ. Usually the question related to *life after death,* and not how becoming a Christian would make a difference *today.* When the person could not give a satisfactory answer,. a memorized presentation would be given, the person would pray to receive Christ, and *the visitor would move on to the next house.*

As a result, the church world is currently filled with gospel tracts, evangelism training courses, etc., which encourage two *strangers* (one a Christian, the other a seeker) to discuss God's plan of salvation without ever bothering to *know* one another. Unfortunately, this is often done without any *intention* of the Christian "soul winner" developing a closer relationship either before, during, or after the conversion experience. Note that the emphasis of such visits always deals with *life after death,* not life *today.*

Because the traditional church neither understands nor teaches "body life," the only thing it can offer a new Christian is membership in an *institution* called "church." If the church is developed around mass meetings and impersonal Bible studies, there is no need to become intimate with those being told about Christ's love. Evangelism is just another program of the impersonal church, and their approach to evangelism is also impersonal.

A TRUE STORY...
One Singaporean said to three Christians eating in a hawker's stall, "Do you happen to be Christians?" They asked, "What makes you think so?" He said, "Well, you seem to be quite different from most people I know. That makes me think you are Christians. But, you don't act like the rest of them I have known." They asked, "Really? How did the other Christians act?" He said, "Like they were tigers perched in the tall grass beside the road, ready to spring on me with their claws!"

You are *not* encouraged to become a "salesman" for the gospel in this equipping course, simply transmitting data to someone who "buys" your product. Instead, we must realize that the *true* gospel is *always a relational gospel.* (That's why the Father sent His son to the earth.) Our task is *not* to get others to agree that four or five thoughts are correct, pray a prayer, and then go to heaven at death.

No! Our task is to bring an unbeliever into a *twofold relationship:* first, with Christ; second, with Christ's body—a Shepherd group. Being a Christian is more than preparation for eternity: *it's a better way to live right now.* The Christian world suffers today from millions of unattached Christians who are like dismembered parts of a human body that cannot function because they are not alive in a relationship with the other "body parts." Their "salvation" is not received until they die. That's not what Christ intended!

We are saved for all eternity as we go to the cross and exchange our sinful life for Christ's atoning life. Immediately following that, we are to enter into a *continuing salvation* in which we are set free from the bondage of sin in this *present* life. This requires a *double relationship* to be established at Calvary: one with Christ, and one with the other members of His body.

LET'S READ I CORINTHIANS 14:24-25:

> . . . if . . . an unbeliever . . . enters, he is convicted by all, he is called to account by all; the secrets of his heart are disclosed; and so he will fall on his face and worship God, declaring that God is certainly among you.

In this passage, we see that a *relationship* with believers should first be established. The presence of Christ was so powerful in the lives of early believers that the unbeliever developed a deep desire to become part of their life together.

What are the characteristics of a person who is seeking for an answer to life and its problems?
(Check the ones you feel are true.)

☐ **A bored expression when Christ is mentioned.**

☐ **A desire to share personal problems or concerns.**

☐ **A willingness to listen as you share your testimony.**

☐ **Openness to doing things with you, being with you.**

☐ **Such a heavy schedule that there's no time for you.**

☐ **A keen interest in what the Bible teaches about Jesus.**

☐ **Deeply moved by your Shepherd group's prayer life.**

Which of these comments could you use to "probe" for the responsiveness of an unbeliever? (Underline your choice.)

"Have you given much thought recently to spiritual matters?"

"Let's talk about Jesus for a moment. Would you share with me what you know about Him, and what you would *like* to know about Him?"

HERE ARE SOME TIMES WHEN IT'S APPROPRIATE TO SHARE THE WAY TO BECOME A CHRISTIAN...

- When the Holy Spirit has come to join you, and the person has a desire to talk about Jesus and His death on the cross for us.
- When your relationship has bonded you together as true friends.
- When you realize that, in spite of comments about a previous experience, the person really doesn't understand what it means to be a true Christian and needs Christ in his/her life.

THE PLAN OF SALVATION...

On the opposite page, a sample diagram is given. Use it as your Equipper uses it, as a graphic way to explain the plan of salvation. *Now, get acquainted with a simple but powerful way to present the plan of salvation!*

THE DIALOGUE...SUGGESTED CONVERSATION

Note: while the following dialogue is prepared to help you think through what you might say when using the diagram, it's not meant for you to memorize. If you become familiar with it, you will do best using your own words in the flow of a heart-to-heart sharing time, rather than using a prepared formula. In real life, the thoughts related to this diagram may be presented in a different sequence, or at more than one time. Let the Spirit lead you!

1. INTRODUCTION

"I want to thank you for the opportunity to come by and visit with you. I'd like to share a little bit about myself..."

(DO SO—TAKE TIME TO BUILD A "TRUST" RELATIONSHIP...)

2. PRESENTATION

(NOTE: SENTENCES PRINTED IN BOLD TYPE ARE QUESTIONS YOU WILL ASK. ALWAYS WAIT FOR AN ANSWER TO THESE QUESTIONS.)

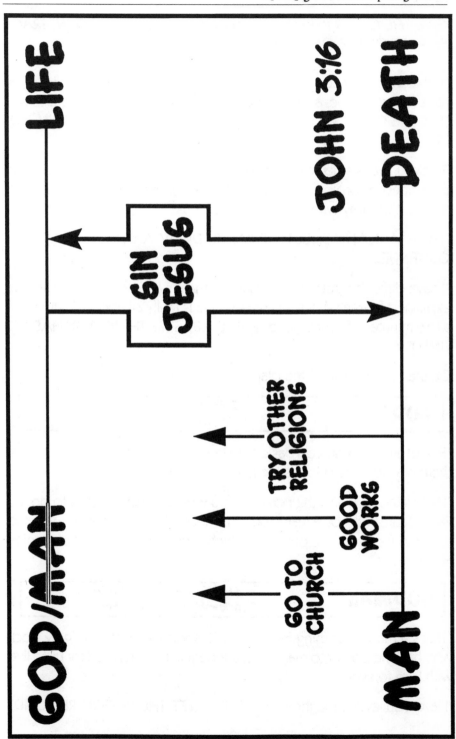

GIVE THE OTHER PERSON PLENTY OF OPPORTUNITY TO INTERACT. BEWARE OF THE ONE-WAY LECTURE APPROACH!

"Could we speak about the meaning of life? I'd like to ask you what you have found it to be, and then perhaps you would let me do the same." (LET THE OTHER PERSON SHARE HIS VIEWS ON THE MEANING OF LIFE.)

"Like you, I've pondered over this also. And then I ran across a little diagram that helped me put together answers that have changed my whole existence. Would it be okay with you if I draw it for us?"

USING A BLANK SHEET OF PAPER, DRAW A DIAGRAM AS YOU CONTINUE...

"I have difficulty grasping things when there's a lot to see. This diagram explained for me what scripture says life is really all about. Could I take a few minutes of your time to do that?" (BE SURE THE PERSON HAS THE TIME!)

On the top left side of the blank paper, write...

GOD ✍	**STEP 1:** *God created us.*

"First of all, let me share a basic truth that most people will agree to: that there is a God, and God is eternal."

"He has the right and the power to do whatever He chooses to do. I'd like to share with you a marvelous truth about God. He created man, and made us for a specific purpose, which is to have fellowship and enjoy Him forever."

GOD/MAN ✍	**STEP 2: Man made to have** *fellowship with Him forever.*

"That's a marvelous thing for us to think about—that an Almighty God, who had the power to make us in the beginning, intended for us to live with Him forever."

"Have you ever thought about that?" (LET THE PERSON RESPOND)

"If God created us, and if He wanted us to live with Him, then we have a problem. I don't mind sharing with you that many things happened in my life to make me know I was apart from God."

"But the beautiful thing about the way He created us is that He breathed His spirit into man, and gave us the right to choose— to make decisions by ourselves."

GOD/MAN   **LIFE**✍

STEP 3:
God intended for us to have a relationship with Him. He breathed His Spirit into us. We're not robots. The choice is ours! Man chose to do his own thing, make his own choices.
WHO WERE THE FIRST PERSONS TO DISOBEY? (Adam and Eve)

"God did not make us robots. I'm glad He didn't, because He made us in His own image, and we can choose whatever we'd like to do with our lives. The sad news is that man chose to do his own thing! Thus, he chose to separate himself from God."

GOD/~~MAN~~✍   **LIFE**

STEP 4:
By his own choice, man is separated from God!

MAN✍

"God is perfect, and He intends for us to have perfect worship and perfect fellowship with Him."

"You've probably heard the story about the first act of disobedience. Have you heard enough about the Bible that you could share with me the story that indicates that man chose to do what he wanted to do?"

(LISTEN CAREFULLY AS THE ACCOUNT OF ADAM AND EVE IS SHARED WITH YOU)

"God had His own reasons for not wanting them to eat of the fruit of the forbidden tree. Basically, He said: 'You can do anything you want to do, but here is something you shouldn't do'—and let me explain that any time God asks us not to do something, it's never to punish us. He always does so because it's for our own good. So, man chose to make his own decision; what did he choose to do?"

(LISTEN TO THE ANSWER)

"Right! That caused a big separation. At that time, man was no longer perfect before God. He had disobeyed God. That is the point where man separated himself from God. That 'separation' can be called lots of things, but there is one word that we all seem to relate to—a word that accurately describes our separation from God..."

GOD/~~MAN~~   **LIFE**

SIN

STEP 5: Explain difference between SIN and SINS. God's way rejected!

MAN

"That word is 'SIN.' Sometimes we get caught up in trying to describe 'SINS,' and we make lists of 'bad' things. But we are not talking now about *actions* when we use the word 'SIN.' Instead, we are talking about that thing within us that basically says, 'I want to do my own thing.' "

"Have *you* experienced that in your life? Have *you* wanted to do your own thing?" (LISTEN TO THE ANSWER)

"I'd like to share with you that this was the case with me. And, it's that way with *everyone*. The Bible tells us that *all* of us choose to follow our own way, rather than obeying God's way."

"Let's think about another point. There's something in each one of our hearts that says, 'I'd like to be right with God!' In those days when I knew

I wasn't right with God, I wanted to be. Do you remember I told you a moment ago that God created man in His own image? That inner spirit of ours, created to know Him, has been separated from Him, and it longs to go back to God."

"If man is separated from God, and He intends for us to have life, what is the opposite of life?"

(THE ANSWER: DEATH)

"This is the big dilemma: God loves us and created us, and desires to have fellowship with us forever. Man is separated from God by sin, and the result is that man no longer can have life, but has death. That's what we have to look forward to."

GOD/MAN————————————————☜ **LIFE**

SIN

MAN————————————————☜ **DEATH** ☜

STEP 6: The opposite of LIFE is DEATH—the result of sin. Yet, man has a spirit that longs to go back to God!

Pause here! Before you continue, *review* the first six steps. You have been developing simple truths that *must* be understood in order to fully understand how to become a Christian. Which of the six steps do you need to review at this point?

CHECK LIST:

STEP 1: ☐ OK ☐ NEEDS REVIEW
STEP 2: ☐ OK ☐ NEEDS REVIEW
STEP 3: ☐ OK ☐ NEEDS REVIEW
STEP 4: ☐ OK ☐ NEEDS REVIEW
STEP 5: ☐ OK ☐ NEEDS REVIEW
STEP 6: ☐ OK ☐ NEEDS REVIEW

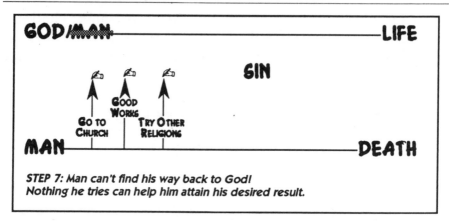

STEP 7: Man can't find his way back to God!
Nothing he tries can help him attain his desired result.

"Let's say this past Sunday we decided we wanted to get back to God. So we go to church. We think, 'Well, God's at church—so I'll go to church.' Many people do that."

"Another thing that some of us do is to decide we ought to give something to other people. So we do good works, try religions (we delve into religions about pyramids, about birds, all kinds of things)."

"Through the ages, man has tried to find a way to go back to God. The sad news is that man can never go back to God on his own! No matter how good we are, or how many churches we go to, or whatever good works we do, we can never go back to God."

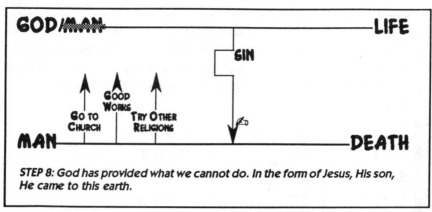

STEP 8: God has provided what we cannot do. In the form of Jesus, His son, He came to this earth.

"But, God loved us so much that he did a marvelous thing for us. One day He chose to live as a human on this earth. He came to this earth in the form of Jesus Christ, His only Son."

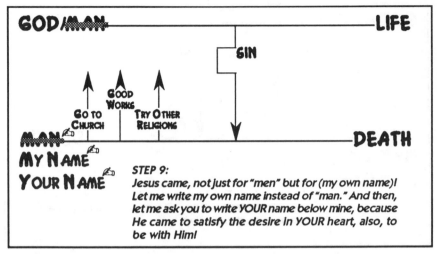

"I'm going to write my name where it says 'Man.' God created me. Here—you take the pen and write your name there, too."

(LET THE PERSON WRITE HIS/HER NAME BELOW YOURS)

"Jesus lived among men for 33 years. He lived a perfect life. He had no sin. At age 30, He declared Himself publicly to be the Son of God, and He went about teaching all the truths that came from God. And we know what happened to Him: He was crucified, nailed to a cross, and He died."

We've just come to an important point in our sharing time. How were you, yourself, impacted by writing your own name in this developing diagram?

☐ **I was deeply moved.**

☐ **I recalled my own conversion experience once again.**

☐ **It gave me a deep desire to share this with someone!**

How do you think an unbeliever will be impacted when writing his/her name below yours?

_____

_____

_____

_____

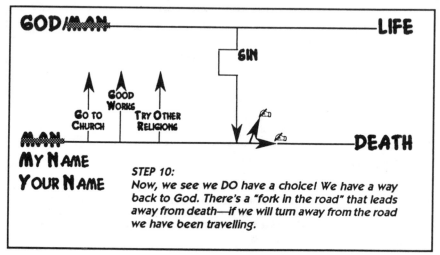

STEP 10:
Now, we see we DO have a choice! We have a way back to God. There's a "fork in the road" that leads away from death—if we will turn away from the road we have been travelling.

"Now, we come to the Cross of Jesus Christ (DRAW ARROWS), and we have to decide: are we going to accept the forgiveness God has given us when Jesus paid for our sins by His death on the cross, or are we going to continue a life on our own? It's just that simple."

"There's a crossroads here!"

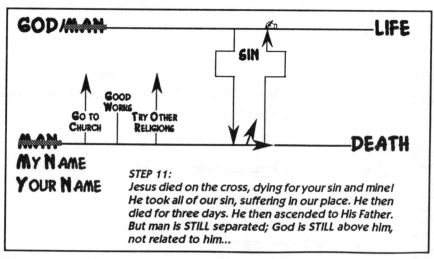

STEP 11:
Jesus died on the cross, dying for your sin and mine! He took all of our sin, suffering in our place. He then died for three days. He then ascended to His Father. But man is STILL separated; God is STILL above him, not related to him...

"Our God died for three days! He then came back to life, and forty days after that He went back to His Father—He ascended back to God."

"Here's the good news! Jesus Christ is back with God, but man is still apart from God."

"Let me ask you a question: do you know any Bible verses?"
(LISTEN TO THE ANSWER)

"Let's look at one that most people know, or at least they've heard about:
Can you quote John 3:16?"

(IF THE PERSON IS ABLE TO DO SO, LET HIM/HER QUOTE IT ALOUD. IF
NOT, FIND IT IN YOUR BIBLE AND ASK HIM/HER TO READ OUT LOUD FOR
YOU.)

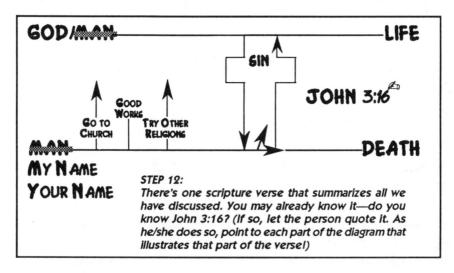

STEP 12:
*There's one scripture verse that summarizes all we
have discussed. You may already know it—do you
know John 3:16? (If so, let the person quote it. As
he/she does so, point to each part of the diagram that
illustrates that part of the verse!)*

"Most people know that verse! So, let's just consider the message of the
one verse that most of us know. Let me show you what this little drawing
says. Look at this—"

"Say John 3:16 again for me:"

(AS IT IS BEING QUOTED, MOVE YOUR PEN THROUGH THE VARIOUS
SECTIONS OF THE DIAGRAM)

(Interrupt at "only begotten Son")

"*Who* was His Son?" (JESUS CHRIST)

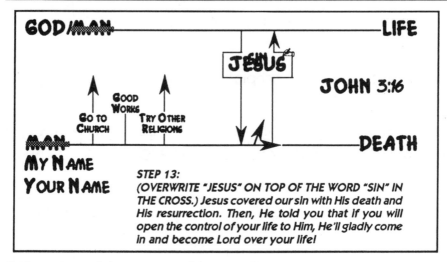

(Write "Jesus Christ" on top of the word "SIN")

(THE PERSON RESUMES QUOTING THE VERSE...)

"Now, let's make this more personal! Instead of talking about mankind, do you mind if I talk about me right here?"

"Now, let's read it again: 'For God so loved (USE YOUR OWN NAME) that He gave His only begotten Son, Jesus Christ, that if (YOUR OWN NAME) would believe in Him, (YOUR OWN NAME) would not die, but have eternal life'."

"Is that what that verse says?" (WAIT FOR ANSWER)

"Now, here's the good news. This same Jesus not only came to earth, and went back to the Father, but He told us that if we will open the door of our heart, He will come in. He will live with you, and stay with you forever. Now, isn't that amazing? God, who created us and died for us, now wants to live in our hearts. He wants to take up residence and live with us."

"Therefore, what God intended takes place today on this earth. God intended for God and man to be together in fellowship. We can have fellowship with God by having Jesus in our heart."

"Here's what happens: each of us must understand that we have SIN that separates us from God. And, we have to deal with this sin as we discussed. We can't deal with it by going to church. Jesus—*not the church*—paid for our sins."

"I would like to ask you: have you ever come to a point in your life where you allowed Jesus Christ to come into your heart, to live inside of you?"

(WAIT FOR ANSWER: "NO, I'VE NEVER DONE THAT")

"Then you are at this crossroad." (POINT TO IT IN THE DIAGRAM.)

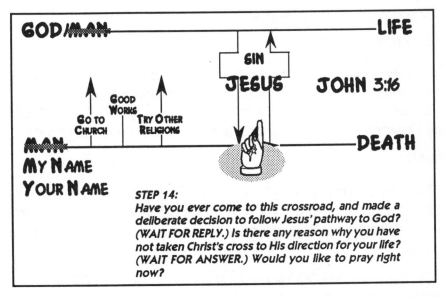

STEP 14:
Have you ever come to this crossroad, and made a deliberate decision to follow Jesus' pathway to God? (WAIT FOR REPLY.) Is there any reason why you have not taken Christ's cross to His direction for your life? (WAIT FOR ANSWER.) Would you like to pray right now?

"Let me share with you the report that one time I was right there, and I saw vividly that if I remained apart from God I'd have 'death'—but I wanted Life! I prayed this prayer: I said, 'Lord Jesus, I know that I'm a sinner. Thank you for dying on the cross for my sin. I invite you to come into my heart now, and take control of my life, and cause me to become the kind of person you want me to be.' At that point, I chose to turn from 'this' way and go 'this' way." (POINT TO THE TWO DIRECTIONS AT THE CROSSROADS IN THE DIAGRAM.)

"Is there any reason why you would not want to choose to go that way today?"

(WAIT FOR ANSWER: "I WOULD LIKE TO DO THAT")

"Then, what you need to do is to pray from your heart, and pray with your lips, and tell God that you accept Him as your Savior and Master. Now, my prayer went like this: 'Lord Jesus, I know that I am a sinner...' "

"Do you know that you are a sinner?"

(WAIT FOR ANSWER)

"Do you know that your sin is separating you from God?"

(WAIT FOR ANSWER)

"Do you want to turn from your sin?"

(WAIT FOR ANSWER)

"The way you do that is to invite Jesus to take control of your life. So, you confess that you are a sinner, and you invite Jesus into your heart to take control of your life, and allow Him to cause you to live the kind of life He wants you to live. Does that express your own thoughts?"

(WAIT FOR ANSWER)

"O.K., why don't we pray right now? I'm going to pray, and when I finish praying, you pray in your own words. You don't have to use my words, because they're not 'magic' words. God hears our hearts more than our words."

(YOU PRAY, ASKING GOD TO HEAR THE PRAYER OF YOUR FRIEND. THEN, LET THE PERSON PRAY).

(FINISH PRAYING, THANKING THE LORD FOR COMING INTO THE LIFE OF YOUR FRIEND AS A RESPONSE TO THE PRAYER.)

"Now, one of the first things we need to do is to tell someone else what we have done! Who is your closest friend—the person you talk to the most?" (GET ANSWER)

"When do you expect to see him/her again?"
(GET ANSWER)

"Why don't you let me go with you to meet your friend, and pray for you as you share with him/her what you did today?

(GET ANSWER)

"Let's review together what you will say about what you did today, in the way you will share it with your closest friend. Pretend I'm that friend! Share with me what you will say..."

"Wonderful! *Share that,* with the same joy I've just observed in you as you related it to me! Let's share a brief prayer of thanksgiving right now. I'm going to pray first. Then, I'd like to ask *you* to pray for God's guidance as you share your testimony for the first time."

Do you realize what this final step will do for the new believer?
(Check appropriate conclusions)

☐ He/she has selected an *oikos* (close friend or relative) to tell about Jesus.

☐ He/she has thought through how to share how Christ has become Lord.

☐ Both of the above.

☐ Neither of the above.

...And what has this also opened for *you*?

☐ An opportunity to meet the best friend of your newly committed believer.

☐ An entrance through this contact into the *oikos* (close friend or relative), and opportunity to find other "Type A" unbelievers who may be searching for Jesus.

☐ Both of the above.

☐ Neither of the above.

(Thrilling, isn't it?)

Here's an actual tape recorded quotation from a Christian who is a member of a traditional, non-cell group church. It was used after a person had prayed to receive Christ:

"I want to get back with you and help you get enrolled in a Sunday School class, where there will be other people growing as Christians along with you. You will be contacted about this!"

How do you react to such a detached, impersonal conclusion to the most important moment in a person's life?

_____

_____

_____

_____

You are the link between this new Christian and the body of Christ! You are the one to lovingly bring him/her into your Shepherd group. In all probability, you will become the "Equipper" of this person in the days ahead.

Entering into the life of a new believer in such a personal way is going to be a great challenge to your own walk with the Lord. The Christian walk is totally, completely foreign to your friend. He/she has lived without considering Christ's Lordship for years; old habits are deeply rooted. They will—*because they are habits*—continue to control daily decisions. Your ministry must be a patient, loving one!

In addition, this person is described by Paul as a "babe in Christ." Milk is the diet, and lots of "tender loving care" is the formula that goes in the bottle. The *Arrival Kit for New Christians* is deliberately written for this part of the journey into Christ. Present a copy of it at once. Together, discuss the pages completed each week during the equipping time in your Shepherd group.

Once you have brought another to Christ, you'll never be the same!

PRACTICAL ASSIGNMENT

INSIGHTS...

Think through the presentation until you have fully digested its fourteen steps. Review the areas that are "fuzzy" as you think about them. *(Do this during idle times, like travelling to work.)* When you feel you have grasped the material, practice sharing it with a Christian friend or relative.

THIS WEEK...

1. Review the presentation daily until you are able to understand the various parts of it. (15 minutes a day will be enough time to achieve this.)

2. Visit this week with your Equipper. If the Lord opens the door, share your own personal testimony about what God has done in your life.

A FINAL WORD...

Let's imagine you have to choose a doctor to deliver a baby. What is the *first question* you will want to have answered? Of course, it will be: "How qualified is this doctor?" The answer: "He spent many *years* preparing to deliver this baby!" When God is looking for those to bring unbelievers to "new birth," do you think He will choose Christians who are untrained and not willing to undergo "medical school?" You will have a lifetime of joyful harvesting of others—*if you are willing to take your obstetrical training seriously.*

Insights

Jot down topics you wish to discuss with your Equipper:

UNIT EIGHT
HOW TO LEAD A LOST
PERSON TO CHRIST—II

DO YOU REMEMBER HOW YOU FELT WHEN YOU CAUGHT YOUR FIRST FISH?

Jesus said, "I will make you fishers of men..." He knew the thrill that every Christian would experience when a lost person is "caught for Him."

Something vital happens in the Christian life when we pass over the barrier of barrenness, and learn first-hand that there is no greater joy in the world than seeing a friend accept Jesus as Lord and Savior. It's important that you "pass the test" of this course, and that you can effectively share the plan of salvation. In this Unit, you'll spend the entire time reviewing.

On the following page, there is another sample of the completely drawn diagram. Refer to it only as you need to do so. Using blank paper, seek to draw it from memory. After your first attempt, check it against the diagram. Then, redraw it until you can do so without missing anything.

When you have accomplished that, review the 14 steps as presented again for you in this Unit. As you do so, draw the diagram and see how effectively you can present the thoughts that go along with it.

Finally, share the presentation with your Equipper when you meet together during the equipping time of your Shepherd group.

This is an important time for you. Before you begin to practice, spend some time in prayer. *This is serious business—eternity may hang in the balance for someone you will meet in the future!*

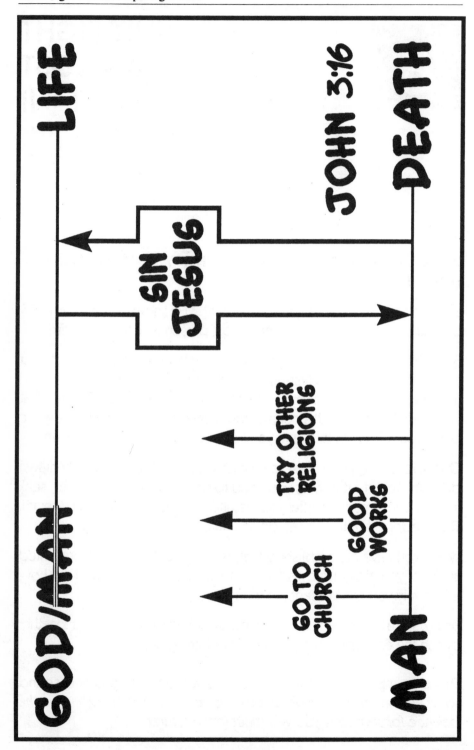

REVIEW...

In this section, you are provided with a condensed version of the materials you have been studying this past week. Try to use it as "prompts" to present the material. Refer to the complete version in last week's materials as you need to do so. Each of the questions you should ask are included in this review.

1. INTRODUCTION

Share about yourself;
Build a trust relationship.

2. PRESENTATION

USING A BLANK SHEET OF PAPER, DRAW A DIAGRAM AS YOU CONTINUE...

"Like you, I've pondered over the meaning of life. And then I ran across a little diagram that helped me put together answers that have changed my whole existence. Would it be okay with you if I draw it for us?"

"Could I take a few minutes of your time to do that?"

GOD ✎	**STEP 1:** **God created us.**

GOD/MAN ✎	**STEP 2:** Man made to have fellowship with Him forever.

GOD/MAN	**LIFE** ✎
STEP 3: **God intended for us to have a relationship with Him. He breathed His Spirit into us. We're not robots. The choice is ours! Man chose to do his own thing, make his own choices.** **WHO WERE THE FIRST PERSONS TO DISOBEY?** *(Adam and Eve)*	

GOD/~~MAN~~ 🖎   LIFE

> STEP 4:
> By his own choice, man is
> separated from God!

MAN 🖎

"Have you heard enough about the Bible that you could share with me the story that indicates that man chose to do what *he* wanted to do?"

(STORY OF ADAM AND EVE IS DISCUSSED)

"What did he choose to do?"

GOD/~~MAN~~   LIFE

SIN 🖎

> STEP 5: Explain difference between
> SIN and SINS. God's way rejected!

MAN

"Have you experienced that in your life? Have you wanted to do your own thing?"

"If man is separated from God, and He intends for us to have life, what is the opposite of life?"

GOD/~~MAN~~——————————————🖎 LIFE

SIN

MAN——————————————🖎 DEATH 🖎

> STEP 6: The opposite of LIFE is DEATH—the result of sin.
> Yet, man has a spirit that longs to go back to God!

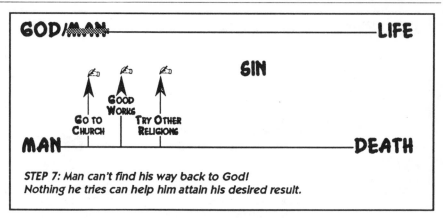

STEP 7: Man can't find his way back to God!
Nothing he tries can help him attain his desired result.

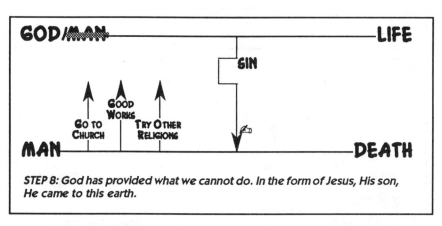

STEP 8: God has provided what we cannot do. In the form of Jesus, His son,
He came to this earth.

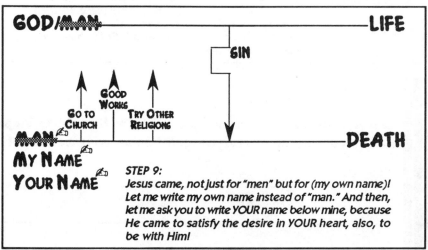

STEP 9:
Jesus came, not just for "men" but for (my own name)!
Let me write my own name instead of "man." And then,
let me ask you to write YOUR name below mine, because
He came to satisfy the desire in YOUR heart, also, to
be with Him!

"Here—you take the pen and write your name there, too!"

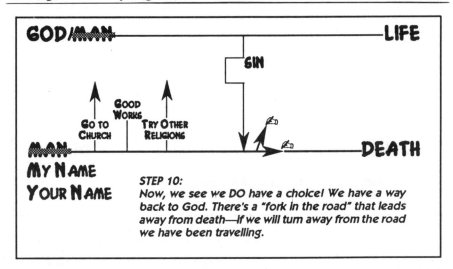

STEP 10:
Now, we see we DO have a choice! We have a way back to God. There's a "fork in the road" that leads away from death—if we will turn away from the road we have been travelling.

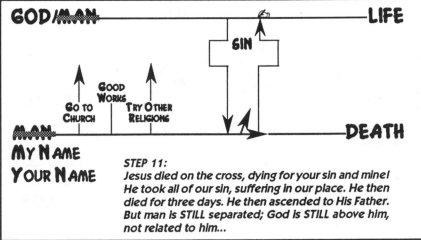

STEP 11:
Jesus died on the cross, dying for your sin and mine! He took all of our sin, suffering in our place. He then died for three days. He then ascended to His Father. But man is STILL separated; God is STILL above him, not related to him...

Check up time!

Can you close your eyes and "see" all of the first eleven steps? Before continuing or reviewing, jot down your weak spots:

_____

_____

_____

"Let's look at a scripture verse that many say is the most well known in the Bible. Perhaps you, yourself, know it by memory. Can you quote John 3:16?"

(IF UNABLE TO DO SO, LET THE PERSON READ IT ALOUD FROM YOUR BIBLE. AS IT IS BEING QUOTED, MOVE YOUR PEN THROUGH THE VARIOUS SECTIONS OF THE DIAGRAM)

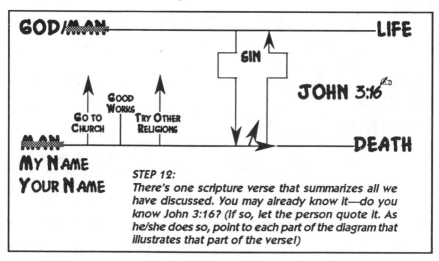

STEP 12:
There's one scripture verse that summarizes all we have discussed. You may already know it—do you know John 3:16? (If so, let the person quote it. As he/she does so, point to each part of the diagram that illustrates that part of the verse!)

(...INTERRUPT AT "ONLY BEGOTTEN SON")

"Who was His Son?"

(Write "Jesus Christ" on top of the word "SIN")

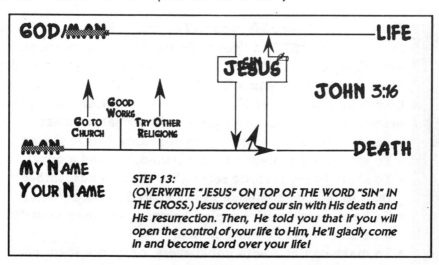

STEP 13:
(OVERWRITE "JESUS" ON TOP OF THE WORD "SIN" IN THE CROSS.) Jesus covered our sin with His death and His resurrection. Then, He told you that if you will open the control of your life to Him, He'll gladly come in and become Lord over your life!

93

"I'd like to ask you: have you ever come to a point in your life where you allowed Jesus Christ to come into your heart, to live inside of you? Is there any reason why you would not want to choose that way today?"

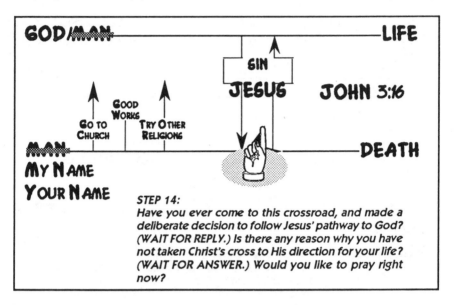

GOD/~~MAN~~————————————————LIFE

SIN

JESUS   JOHN 3:16

GOOD WORKS

GO TO CHURCH   TRY OTHER RELIGIONS

~~MAN~~————————————————DEATH

MY NAME

YOUR NAME

STEP 14:
Have you ever come to this crossroad, and made a deliberate decision to follow Jesus' pathway to God? (WAIT FOR REPLY.) Is there any reason why you have not taken Christ's cross to His direction for your life? (WAIT FOR ANSWER.) Would you like to pray right now?

(YOU PRAY, ASKING GOD TO HEAR THE PRAYER OF YOUR FRIEND. THEN LET THE PERSON PRAY).

(FINISH PRAYING, THANKING THE LORD FOR COMING INTO THE LIFE OF YOUR FRIEND AS A RESPONSE TO THE PRAYER.)

For the rest of your life, you will be useful to the Holy Spirit in bringing unreached lives to Jesus. The brief moments of discipline required of you now are small, compared to the ability that will be yours from now on. Let's check out your Christian values to see if you understand that. Of the choices below, underline the ones you would probably make:
- To watch television, or to pray for those I have visited.
- To telephone someone I have visited, or read a novel.
- To share in my favorite recreation with friends, rather than to include someone I have visited in the activity.
- To have a meal with people I know, rather than to invite a person I have recently visited.
- To make contacts with unbelievers, or ignore them all.

PRACTICAL ASSIGNMENT

INSIGHTS...

Are you asking, "How and when will I use this preparation?" It's simple! Talk to your Lord about the matter. Tell Him, "Master, I'm available. Show me where, and when, you want me to help someone accept Jesus Christ as Lord." *He'll take you up on your offer.* That's what happened to Philip in Acts 8:26ff.!

THIS WEEK...

1. Continue to review the presentation daily, until you are able to share the various parts of it. (15 minutes a day will be enough time to achieve this.)

2. Seek to visit a "Type A" unbeliever this week with your Equipper. Share the presentation as the Holy Spirit gives you an open door.

3. Discuss your visit with your Equipper after you leave. Seek to learn from the suggestions made.

Insights

Jot down topics you wish to discuss with your Equipper:

UNIT NINE
PRACTICUUM—I
DRAWING THE NET

SUGGESTIONS FOR THAT "SPECIAL HARVESTING MOMENT"

As you master the presentation of the plan of salvation, there are some special things you need to know about "drawing the net." In this Unit, you will learn how to handle various responses to it.

These practice sessions are critical to your ministry as a Christian! As discussed earlier, could you imagine anyone asking a *math teacher* to perform surgery? Of course not! A physician would be selected—one who had spent long years learning this skill.

In the same way, our Lord is not going to entrust us with the task of bringing the "Second Birth" (John 3:1-16) to others until we are *prepared* to do so. As a result of your faithfulness in learning these materials, the Holy Spirit will use you as a harvester. He delights in using those who are faithful.

Don't present the plan of salvation as though an insurance agent were making a presentation. His goal is to motivate the individual to take out insurance. *You do not motivate*—you serve the Holy Spirit of God, who alone can draw a person to the cross. If His ministry is not present, the decision to pray the sinner's prayer may be empty of meaning.

Nothing will substitute for observing a person already experienced in harvesting. Make your first soul-winning visits with your Equipper. Observe the way he/she lets the Holy Spirit work.

Then, take your Equipper with you as you seek to lead a person to our Lord. Be willing to accept a frank evaluation when the visit is over. You will soon recognize how to link yourself to the Holy Spirit, becoming His spokesperson.

Pray for those you have already met who need to make this commitment. Pray for the opening to share the message you have learned! Pray for sensitivity to the Spirit's work in other hearts. Pray for clearness as you share God's word!

There are two devices Satan uses to hinder you in your ministry of harvesting: fear of failure and fear of being embarrassed. Which of these two fears do you most often have? In the space below, record your answer and a thought or two about it. Share this as a prayer concern with your Shepherd group when you next meet:

_____

_____

_____

HOW TO DRAW THE NET

You first must discern the individual is obviously under the convicting power of the Holy Spirit! If you know there is a heart-hunger, proceed. Consider the dialogue you have been using in your preparation:

A. PROBE FOR THE SPIRIT'S ACTIVITY

"'I would like to ask you: have you ever come to a point in your life where you asked Jesus Christ to come into your heart, to live inside of you?"

Sometimes you may ask, "You already know many things about Jesus Christ. Have you come to a point where you know you must follow Him, and that you cannot consider living without Him in your life?"

B. PROBE FOR THE PERSON'S DESIRE TO FOLLOW THE SPIRIT'S CALL

"Is there any reason why you would not want to choose to walk in that way *today?*"

C. REVIEW THE KEY TRUTHS ALREADY SHARED

"Do you know that you are a sinner?"

(IF THIS FACT IS NOT ADMITTED, THE DECISION WILL NOT BE SINCERE)

"Do you know that your sin is separating you from God?"

(SEPARATION FROM GOD IS THE VERY REASON WE PRAY FOR SALVATION!)

"Do you want to turn from your sin?"

(ONCE AGAIN, DOES THE PERSON DESIRE TO FOLLOW THE SPIRIT'S CALL?)

"Does a desire to turn from your sin express your own thoughts?"

(AN ALL-IMPORTANT "DOUBLE CHECK!")

How will you know, above all else, that you *must* proceed?
(Check the appropriate comments that, in your judgment, are true:)

☐ **The Holy Spirit will speak to your heart about it.**

☐ **There will be an obvious concern in the unbeliever.**

☐ **You feel it's the time for this person to be confronted with the issue of becoming a Christian.**

☐ **You want to share the plan of salvation that you have worked so hard to memorize.**

D. SHARE THE DIAGRAM AND THE PRESENTATION YOU HAVE STUDIED.

Feel free to adjust it to the situation! Don't feel you have to use it exactly the way you have learned it if your conversation with your friend causes it to go in a different direction.

On occasion, you will find the person has special needs that must be talked about before you can share the truths you have learned. Be patient! Don't let your mind become so tracked to your presentation that you cannot feel and respond to the needs in the life of another person.

After you have completed sharing the basic truths that must be understood for a true commitment to be made, go on to the next step.

As you complete the presentation, how will you know if the person has seriously followed you?

_____

_____

_____

If you get half way through the presentation, and the person changes the subject or is obviously not following you, what's the best approach to take?
(Check the appropriate comments that, in your judgment, are true:)

☐ **Plod on through to the end, and hope his/her attitude will get better as you go.**

☐ **Close your pen, follow the change of subject, and drop the matter at once.**

☐ **Pause and tactfully pray, asking the Holy Spirit to give you both a sense of His presence. Then, ask the person if it is all right for you to continue, or should this discussion be continued at a later time?**

☐ **While these are all possibilities, listen first to the Lord!**

E. TAKE THE PERSON TO THE CROSS

WHEN YOU HAVE FINISHED, SAY, "I CAN'T TAKE YOU BEYOND THIS POINT. MAKING A DECISION TO FOLLOW CHRIST IS A VERY PERSONAL MATTER. SO, WITH YOUR PERMISSION, I'M GOING TO PRAY AND THEN LET YOU MEET THE LORD ALONE."

YOU NOW PRAY, ASKING GOD TO HEAR THE PRAYER OF YOUR FRIEND WHICH WILL FOLLOW. THEN, ASK THE OTHER PERSON TO PRAY AND SURRENDER HIS/HER LIFE TO JESUS.

Here is a moment of great drama! *You* are not the one who saves. You are only the *servant* of the Savior. Therefore, you must take this person to your Master, and get out of the way. Your prayer might sound like this...

"Father, I thank you for the privilege of sharing your word with _____ . Now, let me get out of the way and let him/her talk personally with you."

WITH YOUR HEAD STILL BOWED IN PRAYER, SAY...

"Now, _____ , I have gone as far as I can go with you. You must take the final step to Calvary by yourself. Our Lord wants to meet you there. Let me become a listener as you go to Him. Share your heart with Him. Ask Him to forgive your sin, to become your Savior, and tell Him you are ready for Him to become your Lord and Master..."

Why is it vital that you "get out of the way" and let the Holy Spirit take control of this final step? (Share the response you write below with your Equipper.)

_____

_____

_____

_____

F. WAIT PATIENTLY FOR YOUR FRIEND TO PRAY.

THIS WILL BE THE MOMENT OF DECISION!

G. THREE POSSIBLE RESPONSES YOU WILL FACE WHEN "DRAWING THE NET"...

There are really only three possible responses. All comments made will fit under one of these categories. Be prepared to deal with all three...

ONE OF THREE RESPONSES WILL BE HEARD:

1. "I AM READY."
2. "NO."
3. "I'M NOT QUITE READY TO TAKE THIS STEP."

Perhaps you are thinking, "Wait a minute! If I made sure before I began that the person was ready for this, how will it be that now there might be a "No" or "Not ready" response? (Check the appropriate comments that, in your judgment, are true:)

☐ Some people don't count the cost until it's time to make a final commitment.

☐ Satan has come with full force to keep this person in captivity.

☐ Both of the above statements are true.

☐ Only one of the above statements are true.

EACH ONE OF THESE STATEMENTS REQUIRES A DIFFERENT RESPONSE FROM YOU:

1. "I AM READY."

It's not unusual for the person to take several moments to prepare to pray. It's a significant event! Time is important in thinking it through! Simply *pray* in this period of silence. The person will then pour out a prayer of repentance, asking for Christ's forgiveness and His salvation.

FOLLOWING THE PRAYER OF THE SEEKER, YOU THEN FINISH BY PRAYING—THANKING THE LORD FOR COMING INTO THE LIFE OF YOUR FRIEND.

AFTER YOU HAVE FINISHED PRAYING, ESTABLISH THE PERSON'S NEW LIFE IN CHRIST:

A. ESTABLISH THE PERSON'S WITNESS.

Romans 10:9-10 says literally, "If you will confess—and confess—and confess—**and confess** with your mouth . . ." Thus, it's important to help the new believer realize this is not just one private moment of confession, but the *beginning of many confessions.* Here's the way to do this:

ASK, "Who is your closest friend—the person you talk to the most?" "When do you expect to see him/her again?"

"Why don't you share what you did today?"

B. ESTABLISH THE PERSON'S COMPREHENSION OF WHAT HAS HAPPENED.

This next question does two things: it helps the person verbalize what he/she will say when sharing a testimony, and it helps *you* to know if the decision was authentic:

"Why don't you let me go with you to meet your friend, and pray for you as you share with him/her what you did today?

(GET ANSWER)

"Let's review together what you will say about what you did today, in the way you will share it with your closest friend. Pretend I'm that friend! Share with me what you will say..."

If the response clearly shows the person has made a decision, and totally understands what has happened, he/she will be delighted to "recount" what has just happened with you. If the person struggles to verbalize it, it may mean there was not a true *commitment*—the very heart of a true conversion experience. Establish the reality of the conversion, spending whatever time is needed to do so.

Let's remember your own moment of commitment to Christ. Is your memory of it...

☐ **Vivid**

☐ **Fuzzy**

☐ **Cherished**

☐ **Forgotten**

Discuss what you have marked above with your Equipper when you next meet together.

2. "NO."

The individual is now not concerned about the matter. There is no spiritual sensitivity to the things you have said. When invited to pray to receive Christ, there is a refusal, either with a "No" or such excuse-making that you know that "No" is clearly the answer you are being given.

Whatever else you do, don't try to answer excuses given at such a moment as this. You will void the working of the Holy Spirit if you do so, and reduce the time to one of human persuasion instead of hearing God's call.

Something has happened during the time of the sharing you have done. You may be sure that, whatever form it takes, this rejection is nothing less than Satan snatching away spiritual seed that was spread into this life by the scripture you shared. Here are suggestions to help you in such a situation:

A.   ESTABLISH THE PERSON'S COMPREHENSION OF WHAT HAS HAPPENED.

This next question does two things: it helps the person realize what he/she has said, and helps close the discussion gracefully:

"It seems you don't feel the Holy Spirit's strong call to receive Christ as your Lord...am I correct?"

B. CLOSE IN PRAYER.

Without a lot of additional conversation, continue your prayer. Simply thank the Lord for the privilege of sharing these important truths, and ask the Holy Spirit to seal the memory of them in the mind of the person. Don't do any further "preaching" in your prayer—you'll only irritate the person who is listening.

C. TURN IMMEDIATELY TO YOUR "PRAYER LIST."

There's a further step which can be meaningful to both of you. It creates a link between this moment of sharing and the future conversations you will have.

HOW TO PREPARE YOUR "PRAYER LIST."

Using a blank page in the back of your Bible, write "My Prayer List" at the top of it. Have it available at this time:

MY PRAYER LIST

George Palmer

Mary Sweeney

Fred Franklin

ASK, "Would you do me a favor? I have a daily time when I pray for those with whom I have shared the way of life. Would you write your name for me on this list?"

As the person does so, share your appreciation for being able to talk together about spiritual matters on such a deep level. You have now opened a door of prayer to this person. In the future, when appropriate, you can show your friend this page and indicate you are still praying daily for him/her. Your tender concern is an expression that you *really do care* about this decision being made, and that you were not just "making a visit for the church."

Do you remember the rich young ruler who left Jesus after he counted the cost of following Him? What did Jesus do as he made his decision?

☐ **He sought to warn him of the consequences!**

☐ **He let him go to ponder a reversible decision.**

☐ **He turned His back on him, "wrote him off!"**

☐ **He did nothing—*absolutely nothing*.**

3. "I'M NOT QUITE READY TO TAKE THIS STEP."

The person has responded positively, but something is standing in the way of making a decision at this time. There may be a deep sin which has entangled the person's life. The person does not trust you enough to be open with you, to tell you everything that is involved. What can you do?

A. ESTABLISH THE MEANING BEHIND "I'M NOT READY."

This response may be a polite way of saying "No," or it may indeed be a confession that there are problems standing in the way of making the commitment.

Ask, "It seems to me you are struggling with a problem which makes it hard for you to make a commitment of your life to Christ. Am I correct?"

B. SEEK TO UNDERSTAND THE PROBLEM.

Such problems tend to fall into these major categories:

1. Guilt, which the person considers to be unforgivable.
2. An involvement which seems incompatible with becoming a Christian.
3. Pressures from outside which will become even more threatening if a decision is made.

If your friend now trusts you enough to give you further information about these matters, prayerfully seek to use scripture *(not your opinions)* to answer the problems. If you are not given any explanation, continue by saying...

"I would like to show you a scripture. Would you read it aloud for us?"

Turn to Hebrews 11:16 and let the person read it aloud:

"And without faith it is impossible to please Him, for he who comes to God must believe that He is, and that He is a rewarder of those who seek Him."

C. ENCOURAGE THE PERSON TO PRAY THE "SEEKER'S PRAYER"

This verse explains that God will respond to those who confess they are seeking to find Him. Suggest that it might be appropriate to take this verse literally, and to tell the Father of this desire...

ASK, "Would you be willing to tell the Father you have a deep desire to become His child, and ask Him to help you make that commitment soon? Your prayer would be, 'Lord Jesus, I'm not able just now to give my life to you, but you know I'm seeking you. Please help me to come to that moment when I will be able to accept you into my life and enjoy your friendship.' "

D. CLOSE IN PRAYER; THEN ASK HIM/HER TO SIGN YOUR PRAYER LIST.

As in the previous example, let the person know of your continued prayer for him/her. Your closing prayer, following praying the "Seeker's Prayer," should be a confirmation of your love and your continued concern.

A FINAL WORD...

Remember: you cannot do what the Holy Spirit has not made possible! He is sovereign in moments when unbelievers are confronting Christ's claim of Lordship. He is the one who opens blind eyes, who causes deafened ears to hear the voice of the Son of God. When He is actively working in a heart, it is quite obvious. When He is not working, only the spiritually dull Christian would seek to pressure a person into a decision. Don't be guilty of that! Such "decisions" have no life following them. Church rolls are cluttered with names of persons who "prayed a sinner's prayer," and who made no heart commitment to go along with it. An authentic decision will result in the life of Christ dwelling within the person. There are no substitutes!

While some people make excuses for refusing to accept Christ, most of them have fear in their hearts which slows them down. List two or three areas of fear that might cause a person to say, "I'm not ready." Share your answers with your Equipper:

_____

_____

_____

_____

DON'T ABANDON THE PERSON AFTER YOU HAVE MADE THE PRESENTATION!

After you have shared with a person, it's crucial to continue the relationship. If you don't, the individual will feel your "concern" wasn't genuine, or that your friendships are limited only to those who accept Christ. Some unbelievers have become hardened by the shallowness of Christians who "care" only long enough to present the plan of salvation!

TIME IS AN IMPORTANT FACTOR IN COMMITMENTS TO ACCEPT CHRIST AS SAVIOR AND LORD!

Perhaps weeks, months, or even *years* later, your ministry to persons who rejected or delayed making a decision will finally be completed. Your continued contacts will strengthen the Word of God you have presented to them.

HERE ARE SOME SUGGESTIONS FOR CONTINUING THE CONTACTS:

1. Send a card from time to time.
2. Make a phone call from time to time.
3. Visit the person.

THE MOST EFFECTIVE WAY OF ALL...SHARE GROUPS!

Share Groups are designed to cultivate and develop the unbeliever's concern for becoming a Christian. They often meet for several weeks before friends accept Christ as Lord. In the various stages of growth, the unbeliever will move from Share group topical discussions to Bible study, using *THE WAY HOME* New Testament. It is always a moment of joy when the sowing and cultivating results in a decision for Christ. After you have gained some experience in visiting and have won someone to Christ, you will be eligible to take the next equipping part of your journey: TOUCH BASIC TRAINING—and become a part of a Share Group team. Discuss this with your Equipper.

PRACTICAL ASSIGNMENT

INSIGHTS...

Review the three Responses, remembering what they are and how to respond to them.

Mark a blank page in the back of your Bible, making it "My Prayer List."

THIS WEEK...

1. Continue to review the three Responses until you can deal with all of them with confidence.

2. Continue to visit with your Equipper. Make the Gospel presentation as the Lord opens the way to do so. Discuss your presentation with your Equipper after you leave the unbeliever. Seek to learn from the critique how you might be more effective in the future.

3. Follow up on all the people you have visited since starting this training who have not yet made the appropriate commitment. Do this either with a card, a phone call, or a personal visit. *Let them know you care!*

4. Visit with one of the Team members from our Share Groups. Learn from them how this ministry might be used to cultivate unbelievers who do not respond positively to the presentation of the Gospel message.

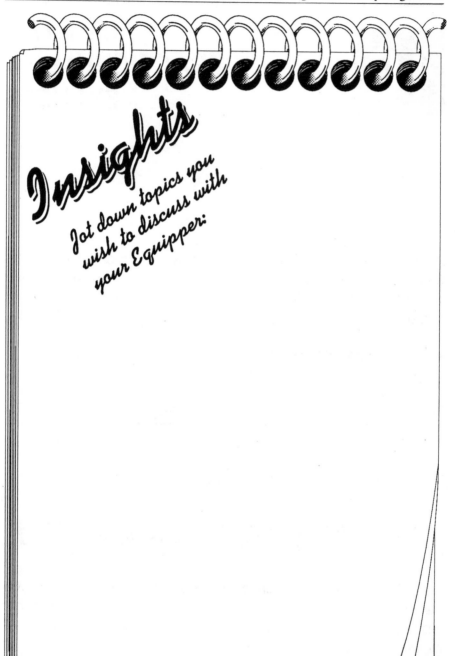

Jot down topics you
wish to discuss with
your Equipper:

UNIT TEN
PRACTICUUM—II
EXCUSES

As you finish sharing the Presentation, a few will respond with excuses for not accepting Christ as their Savior and Lord. Knowing how to deal with them in advance will help you to be more effective in your harvesting ministry.

POSSIBLE WAYS TO HANDLE EXCUSES

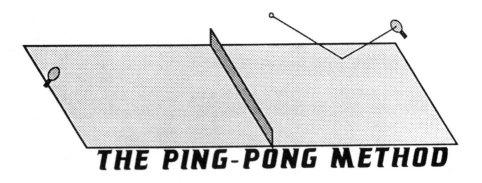

THE PING-PONG METHOD

Using this method, you begin to trade answers about the excuse: you *answer* the excuse, the person answers *your* answer, you answer *that* answer.......until someone drops the ball. There follows a moment of mutual embarrassment!

Even using scripture to answer an excuse may be incorporated as a part of the "ping-pong" method. It will have little effect without the convicting work of the Holy Spirit.

EXAMPLE:

A farmer was asked one day by his neighbor to loan him a rake. He replied, "I can't. I'm going to town!" His wife overheard his reply. After the neighbor left the area, she said, "That was silly! How can you use the rake if you're going to town?" He replied with a grin, "When you don't want to loan your rake, one excuse is as good as another!"

This method pits the intellectual prowess of each person against the other. The excuse causes the Christian to quote sources and use logic to overpower the other person. Instead of achieving this objective, the excuse-giver draws upon *other* sources, uses "better" logic, and the debate is on. Unfortunately, there is no jury to decide who has the better case. The situation deteriorates, hostility arises, and opportunity to share with each other in the future is destroyed.

Avoid this method at all costs. The same mistake is made using this method as with the last one. Excuses are never intended to be answered. They are a polite way to say, "No, thank you!" An excuse-maker is embarrassed when the other person is not smart enough to recognize this, and persists in pressing the issue.

AVOID THESE FIRST TWO METHODS!

You may triumph in the discussion over the other person, but you'll never reach him/her for our Lord. There's a better way. It's the way of the "servant-Christian" (Matthew 20:25-28). Respect the dignity of the other person. Share in a way that is sensitive to the activity of the Holy Spirit.

Let's look at this proper, sensitive way...

The only sensible way to handle excuses is not to answer them at all! Instead, seek to determine the real issue which has prompted the excuse.

EXAMPLES:

Excuse: "I don't understand enough about the Bible to make a decision like this. I want more time to study before making up my mind."

Answer: "Would it help you to share with me the conditions which hindered you from reading the Bible in the past?"

Excuse: "This is really interesting, but I want to be by myself when I do this..."

Answer: "Can you share with me why being alone when you do this is important to you?"

Probe! Ask questions! Seek to find the underlying basis for this camouflage!

A TRUE STORY...
Jim was 29 years old. He said to a witnessing Christian, "I will never become a Christian because I will never believe there is a hell!"

 HOW WOULD YOU RESPOND?

_____

_____

DID YOU ANSWER JIM'S EXCUSE, OR DID YOU PROBE?

Many would seek to "reason" with him about the reality of hell. To do so is to fall into "The Great Debate!" No...*probing* is needed. *Why* did he make that statement? Of all the comments possible, why has he chosen the problem of hell? *There's more to this than the surface objection explains!*

MORE ABOUT JIM...

He loved and respected his father who had died one year earlier. As far back as Jim could remember, his dad had searched through the writings of world religions, looking for truth. Prior to his death, his father had told his son he had rejected *all* religion. He died without any form of faith.

Aha! The Probe Method uncovered the deeper issue: if Jim adopts a Christian belief, he feels he will eternally reject his own father...a man he loves deeply, still in grief over his death. By rejecting Christianity, he seemingly "spares" his father an eternal separation from God.

What can be done to reach him? Perhaps a comment like this would be appropriate:

"Jim, I know you have a strong distaste for hell. Do you know that God despises it even more than you or I do? Let's think again about John 3:16. It says that whoever believes in His son SHALL NOT PERISH, BUT HAVE EVERLASTING LIFE! Is that not what you desire for yourself—everlasting life?"

FIVE PROBE PRINCIPLES

1. DELIBERATE—DON'T DEBATE

When an excuse is given, probe by asking a question instead of giving a rebuttal: "When did you begin to feel that way?"

2. BE TENDER—NOT TRAUMATIC

Your gentle spirit will be a foundation for the Holy Spirit to minister to the deep need in this life. Having an argumentative spirit will trigger defensiveness in the other person.

3. CONVERSE—DON'T CONFRONT

Avoid confrontation! Study the tactful way Jesus did this in His conversation with the woman in Samaria in John 4:1-26.

4. RESPECT—DON'T REJECT

Lost persons often feel their lack of faith excludes them from being accepted by those who have faith. If your friend feels you consider yourself "better" or "superior" because you have become a Christian, your ministry will be lost. If you show respect and treat the other person as having infinite worth, you will be given the same respect.

5. LOVE—LOVE—LOVE!

"If you cut me up into a hundred pieces, every one would cry out, 'I love you! I love you! I love you!' "

These words, spoken by a Christian to a drug addict brandishing a long switchblade, caused the unsaved man to accept Jesus.

The beginning of your message is, "God so *LOVED* the world..." Don't just *talk* about His love—*be* His love! Display that love in dealing with excuses. It will be more powerful than any answer you may say with your lips.

How does that love manifest itself? God gave us the special chapter about it in I Corinthians 13. Meditate on it. To live this way is not only difficult for humans: it is impossible! That is why Paul reminded us that it is CHRIST Who lives in us. In Him, this love can flow. Apart from him, it cannot.

 **Select from the list below the Five Probe Principles. Underline the ones that are correct:**
LOVE—LOVE—LOVE!
PRESS FOR A DECISION!
DELIBERATE—DON'T DEBATE
DIG, DIG, DIG!
(continued on next page)

(continued from previous page)
CONVERSE—DON'T CONFRONT
DON'T GIVE UP!
RESPECT—DON'T REJECT
BE TENDER—NOT TRAUMATIC

SOME COMMON EXCUSES

1. "I'VE ALWAYS BEEN A CHRISTIAN."

Probe for the source of this excuse:

"According to your understanding, what must one do to become a Christian?"
(Review John 1:12-13)

2. "RELIGION WAS CRAMMED DOWN MY THROAT AS A CHILD, AND I WANT NOTHING MORE TO DO WITH IT!"

Probe for the source of this excuse:

"I sense you resent your parents for forcing you to go to church activities?"
(LISTEN TO ANSWER...)

"How do you feel about God? Is it only your parents you resent, or do you resent Him as well?"
(Be prayerful about the way you proceed from this point...)

3. "I DON'T HAVE ANY REAL FEELING THAT I NEED THIS."

Probe for the source of this excuse:

"Have you had contact in the past with religious groups who emphasized that you have to have a *feeling* before you can become a Christian?"
(Review John 1:12-13, pointing out that the focus is on receiving, not feeling. If there is no change in the person's spirit, be hesitant to pursue the discussion.)

4. "I NEED TO STUDY THE BIBLE AND LEARN MORE ABOUT IT FIRST..."

Probe for the source of this excuse:

"Have you made a decision to begin Bible study at this time? I would consider it an honor to share brief Bible studies with you, using a special New Testament our church has published just for this purpose!"

5. "THERE ARE SO MANY HYPOCRITES IN THE CHURCH. I DO NOT WANT TO DO THIS AND BECOME ONE OF THEM."

Probe for the source of this excuse:

"I sense you have some real hurts about people who go to church and who are not all they claim to be. Can you share with me the one that is most significant to you?"
(Listen to the answer. It may be a deeply emotional experience for the person to verbalize this hurt.)

If the excuse has truly been caused by hypocritical conduct, you may wish to say,

"I hurt with you about this. Let me show you how Jesus felt about hypocrites: let's read Matthew 23:13-15. *(Read it aloud...)* Do you feel our Lord Jesus has the power to enable you and me to follow Him without becoming a hypocrite?"

By temperament, are you patient with those who differ with you? Or, do you become insistent that your plans be followed? Take this little test...(Underline your answers.)

☐ **Normally, I'd avoid dealing with excuses like these.**

☐ **I feel I can easily love a person making excuses.**

☐ **It damages my ego for someone to avoid my help.**

☐ **I gain my significance from being successful.**

☐ **I know patience is a part of loving.**

PRACTICAL ASSIGNMENT

INSIGHTS...

We must always remember that when we invade Satan's domain to snatch a victim from his grasp, we have entered spiritual warfare. You will discover that when you come to the *very moment of decision-making,* the most ridiculous interferences will take place: the baby will cry, a friend will walk in, the telephone will ring! Seasoned Christians realize this is simply Satan's way of interfering with what you are doing. Expect it. Prayer is your weapon!

THIS WEEK...

1. Continue to review the three Responses until you can deal with all of them with confidence.

2. As before, visit with your Equipper. Make the Gospel presentation as the Lord opens the way to do so. Discuss your presentation with your Equipper after you leave the unbeliever. Seek to learn from this critique how you might be more effective in the future.

3. Follow up on all people you have visited since starting this training, who have not yet made the appropriate commitment. Do this either with a card, a phone call, or a personal visit. *Let them know you care!*

4. Review the five commonly heard Excuses until you have mastered the responses to them.

Insights

Jot down topics you
wish to discuss with
your Equipper:

UNIT ELEVEN
PRACTICUUM—III
QUESTIONS

As you share the Presentation, certain *questions* may be asked. Unlike *excuses*, these *questions* are sincere probes about areas of the Christian message. In most cases, they must be dealt with before a decision can be made. Often, the person has asked these questions before—and has never received a satisfactory answer.

Be sure to use the "Probe Method" with such questions. You will be far more effective in responding if you understand...

WHY IS THIS PROBLEM IMPORTANT TO THIS PERSON?

Of all the dozens of possible problems, what has caused this one to become significant? For example, a person asks, "Do you think all people who die without Christ will go to hell forever?" Before quickly responding, it's important to have some background!

WHAT PREVIOUS EXPERIENCE IS TRIGGERING THIS QUESTION?

Perhaps this person is thinking about a mother or father who died without personal faith. To accept this teaching, your friend would eternally condemn that parent.

Logically, we know what we believe does not change truth...but people do not always think rationally. Therefore, it is important to know what the impact of your answer will be.

WHAT ANSWERS ARE THOROUGHLY BIBLICAL?

A superficial answer should be avoided! Use scripture for everything you say. If you cannot do so, simply say: "I am not prepared to give you the answer you need. Let me do some digging, and I'll talk with you about that very soon."

As you review the most commonly asked questions in this lesson, underline each scripture verse. In the side margin, write a brief description of the question the verses answer. Using a page in the front or back of your Bible, list these excuses and all the verses you have underlined. Then, when a question is asked, you will be ready to use your Bible!

What is the difference between an *excuse* and a *question*?
(Check all answers you consider to be correct)

☐ **An excuse is a means to avoid making a commitment.**

☐ **A question is a means to find an answer that satisfies.**

☐ **Neither answer above is correct.**

☐ **Both of the above answers are correct.**

HAVE YOU SATISFACTORILY ANSWERED THE QUESTION?

If your answer leaves the person with a furrowed brow or questioning eyes, your response has been inadequate. Probe again! If you need to seek further aid, do so. Become a true servant to your friend.

OFTEN ASKED QUESTIONS:

Why does God permit suffering?

GENESIS 3:1-24: The cause of suffering is man's sin and rebellion.

ROMANS 8:19-22: Man's rebellion causes suffering everywhere. The whole earth groans because of it.

ROMANS 8:18: As long as man rebels against God, suffering will continue.

2 CORINTHIANS 1:3-7: God does not send us suffering; He gives us comfort.

What are the assumptions behind the question, "Why does God permit suffering?" Underline the ones on this list which you feel are true:
1. **God lacks love and compassion.**
2. **God is powerless; otherwise, He would stop suffering.**
3. **If God can't stop suffering, He can't be trusted.**
Do you see what Satan has done? The evil one has sought to destroy man's trust in the love, power, and integrity of God.

How can a man of science believe in miracles?

GENESIS 1:1, JOHN 1:1: God created all matter in the first place.

JOHN 1:3: The God who created all matter in the first place certainly has the power to suspend any natural law at any time.

JOHN 2:11, 23; 4:54: Miracles always have a definite spiritual purpose. They reveal His presence and power.

SCIENCE is a "yardstick" used to measure natural laws. It is totally incapable of measuring anything else. For example, science cannot measure love, hate, evil, or goodness. Such realities are not measurable by scientific procedures. It is also incapable of measuring the suspension of natural laws. Thus, a man of science must accept the limitations of his field.

Write out in the space below your own view of miracles. Discuss this with your Equipper:

_____

_____

_____

_____

_____

_____

How can God condemn those who have never heard about Christ?

ROMANS 1:18-32: Men are condemned because they have rejected God's revelation of Himself through the creation. This revelation is universal. All men everywhere have equally received it.

ROMANS 10:9-15: Men are not lost by not hearing of Christ. They are lost because they rejected His revelation through creation. Men are saved by hearing of Christ. But, hearing of Christ means absolutely nothing to men who have rejected God's revelation through creation. Millions of Americans have heard of Christ, and are lost!

PSALM 8: No person is condemned because he has not heard the Gospel. Because that person has rejected the full revelation of God, brought through creation, he/she is condemned. What God has created is a "picture book," which can be "read" by the most illiterate heathen or the most educated Ph.D.

HEBREWS 11:6: God is obligated to reveal Christ and His salvation to any person who truly seeks Him. In Acts, we see Him responding to Cornelius and the Ethiopian Eunuch by sending Peter and Philip to them.

A TRUE STORY...

Flying over Cambodia in 1974, the pilot of our airplane told us to look out the window and view the war zone 35,000 feet below. We could see puffs of smoke from the cannons, fires, and explosions. A soldier spoke with bitterness to a missionary: "You Christians make me sick. Have you ever seen a child screaming, burned all over with napalm? Why does God allow things like that? I don't want anything to do with Him!" The missionary replied, "Sir, why do you put the blame on God? Are *judges* blamed when they condemn a murderer to a life in prison? Has anyone ever seen God holding a flame thrower? Why not put the blame where it belongs? It is the vileness of *men* that should make you bitter and angry. God gave freedom for man to make choices about life. When he chooses wrongly, and causes suffering, it's unfair to blame God for what happens."

CAN I LIVE THE CHRISTIAN LIFE?

COLOSSIANS 1:21: A logical question for an unbeliever to ask! For a lifetime, this person has been "in charge" of life, and is programmed to carry out all decisions made. This decision will change all that! It is a decision to let Christ take charge.

HEBREWS 4:10: There is a "rest" which is immediately given to the new Christian. It is up to the Christ who comes to live in us to live the Christian life.

JOHN 14:15: The greatest joy of becoming a Christian is discovering the activity of the new King, making all the key decisions. Further, the relationship with Him is one of love, not obligation.

JOHN 14:16: When I become His servant, He gives me a resource I never possessed before.

JOHN 16:13, 2 CORINTHIANS 5:17: When, as a servant, I disobey, the Holy Spirit immediately "notifies" me, and He also makes the strong pull of my old desires disappear.

I JOHN 1:9: Each time I find myself returning to the old pattern of self-rule, I need only "confess" (agree with God) that this is not what is proper, and His rule is again established.

How have you, yourself, found the answer to this question in the time you have been a believer? Thoughtfully write your answer below, and share this with those you visit:

_____

_____

_____

_____

_____

_____

PRACTICAL ASSIGNMENT

1. Continue to review the three Responses until you can deal with all of them with confidence.

2. Follow up on all the people you have visited since starting this training who have not yet made the appropriate commitment. Do this either with a card, a phone call, or a personal visit. *Let them know you care!*

4. Review the "Questions" presented in this lesson, until you are able to deal effectively with them. Mark the scriptures in your Bible as you review them. Add to these scriptures as you work with people who ask additional questions.

Suggestions for marking your Bible:

1. *On a blank page in the flyleaf of your Bible, make a small chart to tell you the first reference in each chain. You can refer to this to help you remember where to start.*
2. *Underline the first verse given in the chain. Jot a tiny note in the margin about the key thought related to it, and the next reference to turn to as you answer a question.*
3. *If you have a Bible with fine India paper, be sure you don't use a pen that will bleed the ink through the paper. Humidity gradually causes this to happen. Many use India ink and a fine pen used for drafting.*

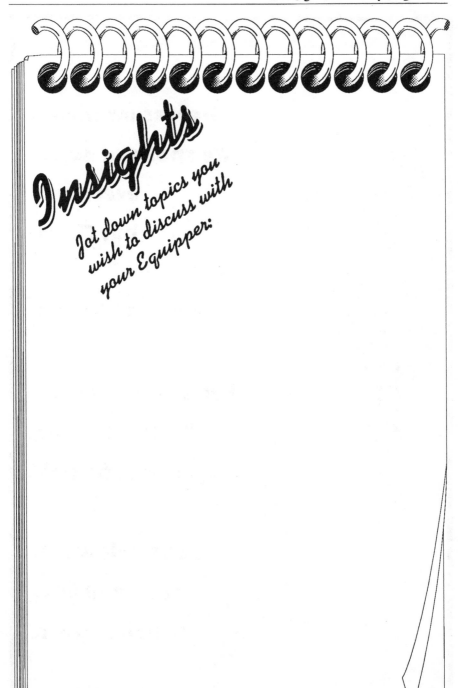

Insights

Jot down topics you wish to discuss with your Equipper:

He was my friend.
We spoke of nearly
everything
but Christ.

I denied him this.

Peter, *you* denied...
Yet lived to say,
"Forgive me, friend!"

I can only weep.
My friend lives
In hell forever.

THE EQUIPPER'S GUIDE

A WORD TO THE EQUIPPER...

Not long ago, you were a visitation intern. Your Equipper during that period poured his/her life into you, showing you how to get started in a simple, basic ministry of the Christian life: reaching "Type A" unbelievers for Christ. During your 11 week internship, you grew in many ways. At the same time, you realized *how much more you needed to learn!*

You will never learn more than by teaching what you have learned! That's why it was important that, once you completed this equipping module, you immediately became responsible for sharing it with a person who needed to be brought into this ministry.

The presence of Christ in your life...the level of your faith in exercising your spiritual gifts...the depth of your prayer life...will all impact your intern as you spend these weeks together. You will grow as much, or more, as the one you are equipping. In doing so, you will learn that the most effective way to be a disciple is to *become a discipler.*

Keeping records is a crucial part of ministering to people. Please stress this with your intern, and be a model of how these records are faithfully prepared and preserved—*and then used.*

Oikos penetration is the key to reaching the lost in great numbers. As you and your partner visit people for the first time, be very sensitive to this fact. Use every means to learn the names of those in the *oikoses* of those you first meet. Heavily emphasize this in your times of sharing with your intern.

This Guide was prepared to help you be effective as you work with your intern. You will meet together during one of the two 20-minute equipping periods in your Shepherd group meeting. Because this is a short period of time, it's very important that you are *thoroughly prepared* to help your visitation intern. The materials in this section are designed to cover the following areas:

1. Review new people given to you for a visit.
How much information do you have about this person? Did a member of the cell group church bring him/her as a guest?

2. Make plans to *telephone* new people and schedule a first visit.
Model how this is to be done by letting your intern listen as you make the first calls. Supervise your intern as he/she makes the first telephone calls.

3. Review names of those already visited, and what has been done by either/both of you to minister to them since you last met.
Remember—the third visit is the one that carries the greatest impact! You probably won't get new names every single week; this gives you more time to follow up on those who have already been contacted.

4. Schedule the time when you will visit together this week.
Consider those who should be approached about accepting Christ as Lord.

5. Discuss the material in the Unit studied, including the questions your intern has answered in each Unit.
If you face a need for deeper discussion than this brief period in your Shepherd group meeting, agree to share more while travelling together to make visits.

May our Lord anoint you for your task of being an Equipper! It's an important way of multiplying your life for Christ. Take it seriously. Bathe your task in prayer.

WORKSHEET—UNIT 1

1. NEW PEOPLE TO BE VISITED:

_____

2. PLANS TO SCHEDULE A FIRST VISIT BY TELEPHONE:

_____

3. REVIEW OF THOSE ALREADY VISITED:

_____

4. SCHEDULE THE TIME TO VISIT TOGETHER THIS WEEK:

_____

5. DISCUSSION OF UNIT 1, INCLUDING THE QUESTIONS:

_____

6. OTHER AREAS YOU WISH TO DISCUSS WITH YOUR INTERN:

_____

_____

_____

_____

WORKSHEET—UNIT 2

1. NEW PEOPLE TO BE VISITED:

_____

2. PLANS TO SCHEDULE A FIRST VISIT BY TELEPHONE:

_____

3. REVIEW OF THOSE ALREADY VISITED:

_____

4. SCHEDULE THE TIME TO VISIT TOGETHER THIS WEEK:

_____

5. DISCUSSION OF UNIT 2, INCLUDING THE QUESTIONS:

_____

6. OTHER AREAS YOU WISH TO DISCUSS WITH YOUR INTERN:

_____

_____

_____

_____

WORKSHEET—UNIT 3

1. NEW PEOPLE TO BE VISITED:

_____

2. PLANS TO SCHEDULE A FIRST VISIT BY TELEPHONE:

_____

3. REVIEW OF THOSE ALREADY VISITED:

_____

4. SCHEDULE THE TIME TO VISIT TOGETHER THIS WEEK:

_____

5. DISCUSSION OF UNIT 3, INCLUDING THE QUESTIONS:

_____

6. OTHER AREAS YOU WISH TO DISCUSS WITH YOUR INTERN:

_____

_____

_____

_____

WORKSHEET—UNIT 4

1. NEW PEOPLE TO BE VISITED:

_____

2. PLANS TO SCHEDULE A FIRST VISIT BY TELEPHONE:

_____

3. REVIEW OF THOSE ALREADY VISITED:

_____

4. SCHEDULE THE TIME TO VISIT TOGETHER THIS WEEK:

_____

5. DISCUSSION OF UNIT 4, INCLUDING THE QUESTIONS:

_____

6. OTHER AREAS YOU WISH TO DISCUSS WITH YOUR INTERN:

_____

_____

_____

_____

WORKSHEET—UNIT 5

1. NEW PEOPLE TO BE VISITED:

_____

2. PLANS TO SCHEDULE A FIRST VISIT BY TELEPHONE:

_____

3. REVIEW OF THOSE ALREADY VISITED:

_____

4. SCHEDULE THE TIME TO VISIT TOGETHER THIS WEEK:

_____

5. DISCUSSION OF UNIT 5, INCLUDING THE QUESTIONS:

_____

6. OTHER AREAS YOU WISH TO DISCUSS WITH YOUR INTERN:

_____

_____

_____

_____

WORKSHEET—UNIT 6

1. NEW PEOPLE TO BE VISITED:

_____

2. PLANS TO SCHEDULE A FIRST VISIT BY TELEPHONE:

_____

3. REVIEW OF THOSE ALREADY VISITED:

_____

4. SCHEDULE THE TIME TO VISIT TOGETHER THIS WEEK:

_____

5. DISCUSSION OF UNIT 6, INCLUDING THE QUESTIONS:

_____

6. OTHER AREAS YOU WISH TO DISCUSS WITH YOUR INTERN:

_____

_____

_____

_____

WORKSHEET—UNIT 7

1. NEW PEOPLE TO BE VISITED:

_____

2. PLANS TO SCHEDULE A FIRST VISIT BY TELEPHONE:

_____

3. REVIEW OF THOSE ALREADY VISITED:

_____

4. SCHEDULE THE TIME TO VISIT TOGETHER THIS WEEK:

_____

5. DISCUSSION OF UNIT 7, INCLUDING THE QUESTIONS:

_____

6. OTHER AREAS YOU WISH TO DISCUSS WITH YOUR INTERN:

_____

_____

_____

_____

WORKSHEET—UNIT 8

1. NEW PEOPLE TO BE VISITED:

_____

2. PLANS TO SCHEDULE A FIRST VISIT BY TELEPHONE:

_____

3. REVIEW OF THOSE ALREADY VISITED:

_____

4. SCHEDULE THE TIME TO VISIT TOGETHER THIS WEEK:

_____

5. DISCUSSION OF UNIT 8, INCLUDING THE QUESTIONS:

_____

6. OTHER AREAS YOU WISH TO DISCUSS WITH YOUR INTERN:

_____

_____

_____

_____

WORKSHEET—UNIT 9

1. NEW PEOPLE TO BE VISITED:

_____

2. PLANS TO SCHEDULE A FIRST VISIT BY TELEPHONE:

_____

3. REVIEW OF THOSE ALREADY VISITED:

_____

4. SCHEDULE THE TIME TO VISIT TOGETHER THIS WEEK:

_____

5. DISCUSSION OF UNIT 9, INCLUDING THE QUESTIONS:

_____

6. OTHER AREAS YOU WISH TO DISCUSS WITH YOUR INTERN:

_____

_____

_____

_____

WORKSHEET—UNIT 10

1. NEW PEOPLE TO BE VISITED:

_____

2. PLANS TO SCHEDULE A FIRST VISIT BY TELEPHONE:

_____

3. REVIEW OF THOSE ALREADY VISITED:

_____

4. SCHEDULE THE TIME TO VISIT TOGETHER THIS WEEK:

_____

5. DISCUSSION OF UNIT 10, INCLUDING THE QUESTIONS:

_____

6. OTHER AREAS YOU WISH TO DISCUSS WITH YOUR INTERN:

_____

_____

_____

_____

WORKSHEET—UNIT 11

1. NEW PEOPLE TO BE VISITED:

_____

2. PLANS TO SCHEDULE A FIRST VISIT BY TELEPHONE:

_____

3. REVIEW OF THOSE ALREADY VISITED:

_____

4. SCHEDULE THE TIME TO VISIT TOGETHER THIS WEEK:

_____

5. DISCUSSION OF UNIT 11, INCLUDING THE QUESTIONS:

_____

6. OTHER AREAS YOU WISH TO DISCUSS WITH YOUR INTERN:

_____

_____

_____

_____

CERTIFICATE OF COMPLETION

This is to share that

_____

has finished the apprenticeship period of eleven weeks, and has brought at least one person to receive Christ as Lord.

We give our hearty endorsement of the Christian growth which has been experienced, and recommend that the next step for our fellowsoldier will be to:

1. Serve as an Equipper of this material;
2. Be trained to minister on a Share Group team.

Endorsement:

_____

Equipper

_____

Shepherd